INTERPRETING THE
BOOK OF
REVELATION

HERMENEUTICAL GUIDELINES,
WITH BRIEF INTRODUCTION
TO LITERARY ANALYSIS

INTERPRETING THE BOOK OF REVELATION

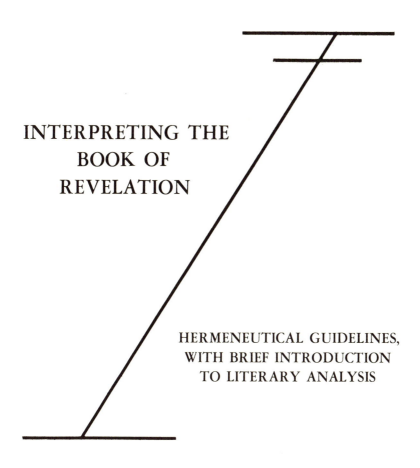

HERMENEUTICAL GUIDELINES,
WITH BRIEF INTRODUCTION
TO LITERARY ANALYSIS

SECOND EDITION

By
Kenneth A. Strand

ANN ARBOR PUBLISHERS

ANN ARBOR PUBLISHERS, INC.   P.O. Box 7249   Naples, Florida 33940

PREFACE

The present book contains a republication of materials originally appearing in *The Open Gates of Heaven,* plus a number of new items. In addition to various revisions in the earlier part of the volume, there has been a fair amount of expansion of material in the main text toward the end of Chapter V and at the beginning of Chapter VI. Also, Essays III and IV in the Appendix are new.

Information regarding the purpose and scope of the present publication is set forth in the Introduction on pages 9-10, as well as in the prefaces to the first and second editions of *The Open Gates of Heaven,* which prefaces are reprinted on page 6. It is hoped that *Interpreting the Book of Revelation* will provide the kind of service afforded by the two editions of its predecessor.

Berrien Springs, Michigan
February, 1976

Kenneth A. Strand

NOTE TO SECOND EDITION

The revisions and additions to this second edition of *Interpreting the Book of Revelation* have been kept minimal (they occur mainly on pages 46 and 78-79 of the text and in the diagram on page 52). Except for a slight relocation of material appearing on pages 78-79 in the first edition, the pagination for material in both editions is identical.

Berrien Springs, Michigan
June, 1979

Kenneth A. Strand

PREFACES TO *THE OPEN GATES OF HEAVEN*

PREFACE TO FIRST EDITION

This small volume is a brief non-technical study of certain basic factors involved in developing a proper hermeneutic for interpreting the New Testament book of Revelation. As such, it takes the risk that most short introductions do: over-simplification. Nevertheless, I hope that what is provided herein will serve a useful purpose as a guide to various hermeneutical considerations which are important in dealing with the Revelation.

It should be stated that subjects such as the date and authorship of the book of Revelation and the historical and geographical backgrounds fall outside the scope of the present study. Important as all these are, they are not vital to the literary analysis which forms the basis for the present publication. Moreover, these matters and others of similar nature are treated in numerous works which are readily available. Further information regarding the scope of the present book is given in the Introduction.

I express my gratitude to my students, who have challenged and inspired me, and who have encouraged me to put these hermeneutical guidelines into print.

Berrien Springs, Michigan   Kenneth A. Strand
November, 1969

PREFACE TO SECOND EDITION

The second edition of *The Open Gates of Heaven* is called "enlarged" for two reasons: (1) the page size and type size have been increased somewhat; and (2) additional material has been incorporated, primarily in the form of two essays in an Appendix. This particular plan for enlargement was chosen in order to provide a more easily readable printed page and to add certain new items of information, while at the same time making as little change as possible in the pagination of the material which appeared in the original edition.

It is hoped that the present modest volume will continue to provide the kind of service that created the demand for its appearance.

Berrien Springs, Michigan   Kenneth A. Strand
October, 1972

CONTENTS

LIST OF MAJOR OUTLINES AND DIAGRAMS

OUTLINES

DIAGRAMS

INTRODUCTION

The New Testament book of Revelation is a book which contains messages of special comfort and hope for Christians. Even the titles of certain recent works dealing with the Revelation, such as D. T. Niles' *As Seeing the Invisible* and Paul S. Minear's *I Saw a New Earth,* give prominence to this thought.[1] One writer has aptly stated that the Revelation "contains so much that is large with immortality and full of glory that all who read and search it earnestly receive the blessing to those 'that hear the words of this prophecy, and keep those things which are written therein' " and also that "one thing will certainly be understood from the study of Revelation—that the connection between God and His people is close and decided."[2] Furthermore, a better understanding of the books of Daniel and Revelation will give "such glimpses of the open gates of heaven that heart and mind will be impressed with the character that all must develop in order to realize the blessedness which is to be the reward of the pure in heart."[3]

However, altogether too often a faulty hermeneutic has been applied to a study of the Revelation. This leads at best to a failure to gain the full meaning and inspiration the book provides, and at worst to gross misunderstandings of the book and its message. In some of the more recent studies on the Revelation there is evidence of a growing emphasis on proper hermeneutics. This is a welcome trend inasmuch as sound interpretational principles are essential for arriving at correct interpretation. The present small volume may be classified as a hermeneutical study rather than an interpretative one. It places main stress on literary features.

It may seem strange that a historian would attempt to deal with literary analysis. However, as a historian I feel that literary context is equally significant with historical context for gaining a correct understanding of any ancient document. As far as the book of Revelation is concerned, a great deal of attention has been given to various historical backgrounds and settings whereas literary context has rarely been given sufficient weight. By "literary context" I mean not only the immediate

---

[1]Niles, *As Seeing the Invisible* (New York, 1961), and Minear, *I Saw a New Earth* (Washington, D.C., 1968).

[2]E. G. White, *Testimonies to Ministers* (Mountain View, Calif., 1923), p. 114.

[3]*Ibid.*

9

textual setting of any statement or symbol in a document, but also such considerations as the following: (1) the literary type or types represented in the document, as these types are to be understood within the framework of the literary milieu; (2) the relationship of imagery, symbolisms, and the like, not only to historical backgrounds and settings but also to literary conventions of the time; and (3) the literary structure of the book, both as a whole and in its various subdivisions.

Each of the foregoing aspects will be touched upon briefly in one or more of the several short chapters which follow. As a beginning point for our study, however, it may be well to glance at various approaches that have been used in analyzing and interpreting the book of Revelation. But before turning to Chapter I, where this will be done, a word of definition is in order for a term which will occur repeatedly throughout our discussion: *eschatology* (and its adjective, *eschatological*). A pure dictionary definition explains the term, of course, as a "study of last things." From the Biblical point of view, and also that of the most common usage today, "last things" of cosmic scope are intended. In a sense, the first coming of Christ ushered in the eschatological age,[4] but there is also a sense in which eschatology is still future.[5] From the standpoint of the book of Revelation, the term "eschatology" will be restricted to the latter sense, inasmuch as it will be placed over against a "history" or "historical era" which encompasses the present age. "Eschatology" as used herein (and unless otherwise defined) will apply, then, to the "last things" of earth's history and to the ushering in of God's judgment and of the apocalyptic kingdom as these are portrayed in the book of Revelation.[6]

---

[4]This is surely implied in certain texts in the gospels, such as Luke 17:20, 21, and is further amplified by the Apostle Paul. Not inappropriate is Oscar Cullmann's remark that "the End-time is already introduced by Christ's resurrection" (*Die Christologie des neuen Testaments* [Tübingen, 1957], p. 213), though in another sense Christ's very ministry ushered it in.

[5] There are, of course, many references throughout the New Testament to a future Kingdom of God, to Christ's coming in glory, and to the end of the age, such as in Matt. 24, 25; Mark 13; Luke 17:24ff.; Luke 21; I Thess. 4:15ff.; II Thess. 1,2.

[6]This definition, it should be stressed, is utilized as a matter of convenience because it relates to the literary structure of the book itself, and that this usage is not to be construed as prejudicial to the fact that the Revelation, like other New Testament literature, recognizes an eschatological aspect to Christ's first coming.

CHAPTER I

APPROACHES TO THE BOOK OF REVELATION

Historically there have been three main approaches in interpreting the book of Revelation: preterist, futurist, and continuous-historical (sometimes called historicist). In addition there are approaches which combine these methods or which present variations of them.

Preterist Interpretation

Preterist interpretation, as the name implies, is one which attributes fulfillment of the messages of the book of Revelation almost exclusively to the past—specifically the past of the Early-Church period. Such, for example, is represented by Luis de Alcazar (died 1613), a Jesuit of Seville in Spain, whose monumental *Investigation of the Hidden Sense of the Apocalypse* was published posthumously in 1614. He and various conservative Protestant writers of later centuries (such as Moses Stuart, I. T. Beckwith, and H. B. Swete) have tended toward an interpretation which sees most of the messages of Revelation fulfilled by the time of Constantine the Great in the 4th century A.D. The main line of preterist interpretation today, however, is that of liberal scholars who see the Revelation as basically a reflection of conditions and events in John's own time.

Preterist interpreters—especially those in the liberal tradition—follow certain hermeneutic principles which are too frequently neglected by other interpreters. Among these principles are careful notation of the historical setting and backgrounds for the Revelation, interpretation of symbols in harmony with the conventional meanings of those symbols at the time of writing, and alertness to the fact that the book of Revelation belongs to a genre of literature called "apocalyptic" (the Revelation is, of course, often called "the Apocalypse").

But there are also objections to the preterist mode of interpretation. For one thing, preterists frequently tend to remove present-day relevance. Perhaps more fundamental from a purely hermeneutic standpoint, however, is the fact that they often do injustice to some of the most basic elements of what may be called the "apocalyptic perspective" and also of what may be called the general "Biblical perspective." The former encompasses, among other things, a broad view or cosmic sweep of history; and the latter includes a special emphasis on on-going history.[1] Preterist interpretation tends too frequently to minimize or negate these basic features.

Futurist Interpretation

The futurist interpretation looks upon the book of Revelation as treating mainly events of the future—not merely John's future but our own. What is undoubtedly the most popular school of futurists believes that most of the events from Revelation 4 onward (at least up to chapter 19) fit within a seven-year period just before Christ's Second Advent. This group, commonly known as dispensationalists or pretribulationists, believes that there is a rapture of the church at a secret coming of Christ seven years prior to His visible second coming. Sometimes they interpret the words of Revelation 4:1 "Come up hither" as being this special "secret rapture."

It seems difficult to find much, if anything, to say favorably of this view. On the other hand, negative considerations often include failure to give due respect to the nature of apocalyptic literature, disregard for the Biblical perspective concerning history, lack of sufficient appreciation for historical backgrounds and settings, and removal of interpretation from the realm of possible scholarly control.

Continuous-Historical Interpretation

The third traditional method of approaching the book of Revelation is the continuous-historical or historicist. This tends to place most of the book of Revelation within the period of history from the time of John to the eschatological climax. There are really two schools of continuous-historical interpretation—what may be called the "straight-line" and what may be called the "recapitulationist."

Numerous interpreters of earlier generations tended to follow the straight-line method, including Adam Clarke, Albert Barnes, and E. B. Elliott. Such interpreters would usually accept the "seven churches" as literal churches of John's day, but would stretch out the rest of the book of Revelation into a continuous line of events happening throughout the Christian centuries. For example, the seals were frequently interpreted as depicting events down to the time of Constantine, the first six trumpets as a description of the barbarian invasions and of the Moslem conquest, the details of chapters 10 and 11 as dealing with the Reformation of the 16th century, et cetera. Even the seven last plagues

---

1 More will be said in this regard in Chap. II.

were often considered as belonging within the historical period (the first plague as representing the French Revolution, for example).

The "recapitulationist" version tends to see the various series of messages—such as churches, seals, and trumpets—as providing parallel treatment or coverages of the history of Christianity from the time of Christ to the eschatological consummation. Often the last chapters of Revelation are considered entirely eschatological, though various interpreters differ on where they divide between historical series and pure eschatology. William Hendriksen, *More Than Conquerors* (Grand Rapids, Mich., 1940), and S. L. Morris, *The Drama of Christianity* (Richmond, Va., 1928), possibly could be classified as recapitulationist continuous-historical, though in some ways they are better classified as "philosophy of history" (an interpretational approach which we shall discuss in a moment).[2] Perhaps the most representative example of continuous-historical interpretation of the recapitulationist variety is Uriah Smith, *Thoughts on Daniel and the Revelation* (rev. ed.; Nashville, Tenn., 1944). He sees the churches, seals, trumpets, and struggle between the powers of good and evil in Revelation 12 and 13 as four parallel historical series depicting developments during the Christian era.

Continuous-historical interpretation of both varieties gives due respect to the apocalyptic and biblical perspectives regarding cosmic scope and historical emphasis. Too often, however, interpreters using this approach have failed to take into adequate account the historical settings and backgrounds both for the entire book and for specific symbolisms used in it. Indeed, there is a tendency among continuous-historical interpreters to ignore the meaning of the message for John's own day and to launch out with private interpretations of the symbolisms. Somehow each interpreter tends to become a "law unto himself," and frequently the applications given to the messages are widely divergent. A comparison of Barnes, Clarke, Elliott, and others, for example, reveals numerous contradictions in the application of symbols. Continuous-historical interpreters also tend at times to carry points to ridiculous fineness of interpretation. For example, B. H. Carroll, *The Book of Revelation* (New York, 1913), page 221, refers to the frogs in Revelation 16 as representing (1) the Council of Trent, (2) Vatican Council I, and (3) "papal encyclicals and syllabuses, particularly those completing the system of Mariolatry." One wonders if Carroll had

---

[2] A summarized form of Hendriksen's outline of the Revelation and a diagram illustrating his approach are given in Chap. IV, below.

written his book today whether he might not have put Vatican II in place of his third choice! Such absurdity in interpretation (unfortunately, among historicists many examples could be cited) has led various scholars to look with disdain upon this approach. It is an approach, however, which does have some real values to contribute if only it is tempered with sound hermeneutic.

Other Approaches

Although the foregoing methods of interpreting the book of Revelation are the traditional and most common ones, certain variations have appeared in recent years. Various terminologies are used to describe them, such as "symbolic," "dramatic," "mythological language," "idealist," "value-philosophy," "recurrent fulfillment," and "allegorical." Among numerous representatives of one or the other of these approaches are E. W. Benson, Raymond Calkins, William Milligan, Paul S. Minear, S. L. Morris, and D. T. Niles. Frequently these approaches will overlap each other as well as embrace either preterist or continuous-historical interpretation (or to some degree both of the latter). Often these special interpretations accept the messages of Revelation as applicable for John's day, but refuse to limit their fulfillment to that era. This is true irrespective of whether wider fulfillments are looked upon as being simply drama, as containing a revelation of ideals, or as having actual historical fulfillment in one way or another.

Instead of treating the many variations, I would simply call attention here to one somewhat embracive approach which might loosely be called "philosophy of history." The particular type of "philosophy of history" which I have in mind correlates in a certain sense with both preterist and continuous-historical interpretation, but it does so in a way that allows for repeated historical fulfillments beyond the writer's own time or beyond any other specific time in history. From a certain viewpoint, this approach may be considered essentially a variation of the continuous-historical mode of interpreting the book of Revelation. As a striking example of the approach I quote a few paragraphs from Ellen G. White, *Acts of the Apostles* (Mountain View, Calif., 1911), pp. 585-589:

> The names of the seven churches are symbolic of the church in different periods of the Christian era. The number seven indicates completeness, and is symbolic of the fact that the messages extend to the end of time, while the symbols used reveal the condition of the church at different periods in the history of the world. . . .

At the time when John was given this revelation, many had lost their first love of gospel truth. But in His mercy God did not leave the church to continue in a backslidden state. In a message of infinite tenderness He revealed His love for them, and His desire that they should make sure work for eternity. "Remember," He pleaded, "from whence thou are fallen, and repent, and do the first works."

The church was defective, and in need of stern reproof and chastisement; and John was inspired to record messages of warning and reproof and entreaty to those who, losing sight of the fundamental principles of the gospel, should imperil their hope of salvation. But always the words of rebuke that God finds it necessary to send are spoken in tender love, and with the promise of peace to every penitent believer. "Behold, I stand at the door, and knock," the Lord declares; "if any man hear My voice, and open the door, I will come in to him, and will sup with him, and he with Me."

And for those who in the midst of conflict should maintain their faith in God, the prophet was given the words of commendation and promise: "I know thy works: behold, I have set before thee an open door, and no man can shut it: for thou hast a little strength, and hast kept My word, and hast not denied My name.... Because thou hast kept the word of My patience, I also will keep thee from the hour of temptation, which shall come upon all the world, to try them that dwell upon the earth." The believers were admonished: "Be watchful, and strengthen the things which remain, that are ready to die." "Behold, I come quickly: hold that fast which thou hast, that no man take thy crown."

It was through one who declared himself to be a "brother, and companion in tribulation," that Christ revealed to His church the things that they must suffer for His sake. Looking down through long centuries of darkness and superstition, the aged exile saw multitudes suffering martyrdom because of their love for the truth. But he saw also that He who sustained His early witnesses would not forsake His faithful followers during the centuries of persecution that they must pass through before the close of time. "Fear none of those things which thou shalt suffer," the Lord declared; "behold, the devil shall cast some of you into prison, that ye may be tried; and ye shall have tribulation: ... be thou faithful unto death, and I will give thee a crown of life."

And to all the faithful ones who were striving against evil, John heard the promises made: "To him that overcometh will I give to eat of the tree of life, which is in the midst of the paradise of God." "He that overcometh, the same shall be clothed in white raiment; and I will not blot out his name out of the book of life, but I will confess his name before My Father, and before His angels." "To him that overcometh will I grant to sit with Me in My throne, even as I also overcame, and am set down with My Father in His throne."

The foregoing is, of course, an application pertaining only to the messages to the seven churches. But although this author nowhere gives a verse-by-verse exposition of the book of Revelation, allusions she makes in various places in her extensive religious writings reveal that the "philosophy-of-history" approach indicated by the foregoing quotation is by no means limited to the messages to the seven churches. For example, an ascription of praise from Revelation 5 is applied in her writings at least five different ways or to five different occasions, as Edwin R. Thiele has pointed out.[3] Other examples could be afforded as well.

This kind of approach gives full recognition to the characteristics of apocalyptic and to the important historical element in the Biblical perspective. It also goes beyond the preterist and historicist views in making the book of Revelation relevant to all time and even to the individual Christian life. Thus, it carries interpretation beyond a mere mechanical historical exposition. There is good reason to question whether any interpretation that fails so to broaden the perspective does not also actually do injustice to the intent of the book of Revelation. But this sort of approach is meaningful; it helps us to realize how the book contains "so much that is large with immortality and full of glory" and why a study of it reveals "that the connection between God and His people is close and decided."[4]

---

[3] Thiele, *Outline Studies in Revelation* (Berrien Springs, Mich., 1949), pp. 100-105.

[4] White, *Testimonies to Ministers,* p. 114; quoted more fully in the Introduction, above.

CHAPTER II

THE BOOK OF REVELATION: ITS LITERARY MILIEU

The book of Revelation, like other ancient written documents, belongs to a certain genre of ancient literature. It uses both the language and literary form current at the time of its writing. In order to approach this book correctly we must, therefore, understand its language and the characteristics of its literary form and structure.

Even a first brief glance at the Revelation will immediately reveal that this document is in the form of a letter. Not only are there letters to the individual seven churches (chapters 2 and 3), but the whole book is one epistle. However, there is another characteristic literary form pervading and permeating this book: the apocalyptic. The closest Bible parallel to the apocalyptic of Revelation is to be found in the Old-Testament book of Daniel, though the prophet Zechariah and certain passages in the synoptic gospels are also apocalyptic in nature. For an understanding of apocalyptic literature—an understanding which is useful as background in dealing with the book of Revelation—, it is well to note some of the extra-biblical apocalypses written shortly before the time of Revelation or approximately contemporary with it. Such would include Enoch literature (the so-called Ethiopic Enoch, Slavonic Enoch, and Enoch materials made available from the discovery of the Dead Sea Scrolls), the Book of Jubilees, the Testaments of the Twelve Patriarchs, the Baruch Apocalypse, II Esdras (IV Ezra), and others (including certain of the Sibylline Oracles). It is beyond the scope of the present publication to provide a description of this literature, but useful sources which may be consulted include R. H. Charles' two-volume *Apocrypha and Pseudepigrapha of the Old Testament* (a standard translation into English); H. H. Rowley, *The Relevance of Apocalyptic* (London, 1944), and D. S. Russell, *The Method and Message of Jewish Apocalyptic* (Philadelphia, 1964). G. E. Ladd in his *Jesus and the Kingdom* (New York, 1964) and its revised and updated version *The Presence of the Future* (Grand Rapids, Michigan, 1974) has also given some valuable insights. Especially helpful for a brief but comprehensive survey of major issues is Leon Morris, *Apocalyptic* (Grand Rapids, Michigan, 1972, 1974). The rather extensive work by Paul D. Hanson, *The Dawn of Apocalyptic* (Philadelphia, 1975) breaks new ground in relating apocalyptic eschatology to the prophetic tradition in Israel but may be too restrictive in its focus on but one aspect of apocalyptic.

Not only, however, does the book of Revelation fall within the scope of apocalyptic literature; it is specifically *Biblical* apocalyptic. It partakes of what might be called the "Biblical perspective." Still further, it is part of the New Testament and partakes of the New Testament outlook.

Nature of Apocalyptic

It is well to outline briefly a few of the main characteristics of apocalyptic literature. The Bible contains, of course, a variety of literary types, each with its own peculiar emphasis. Apocalyptic has its particular emphasis. Whereas, for instance, narrative gives illustration by typical example, wisdom literature emphasizes practicality, and general prophecy stresses ethic, apocalyptic places its main emphasis on destiny. Some of its special characteristics may be listed as follows:

1. *Striking contrasts.* As one reads the book of Revelation, he becomes immediately aware of striking contrasts. There are, for example, people of God and people of the adversary, the seal of God and the mark of the beast, the Faithful and True Witness and the serpent that deceives the world, the virgin and the harlot, the armies of heaven and the armies of earth, the marriage supper of the Lamb and the fowls' supper of the men of the earth, songs of praise to God and cries of agony for rocks and mountains to fall, the fruit of the tree of life and the wine of the wrath of God, the New Jerusalem in glory and Babylon in shame, and the sea of glass and the lake of fire. Apocalyptic generally brings sharply into focus two sides. It makes a clear division between good and evil. Rather than a gradual fusion or blending of one into the other, it portrays a clear line of demarcation.

2. *Cosmic sweep.* Apocalyptic has cosmic sweep or universal scope. It deals with large themes—the great controversy between good and evil, not merely within a limited historical framework but from a viewpoint which unrolls the curtain, as it were, for the whole span of human history.

3. *Eschatological emphasis.* This cosmic sweep is viewed, however, with an emphasis on eschatology. There is an ongoing struggle between good and evil in history, a history which tends even to degenerate as it proceeds in time. But that history is moving toward an end at which God Himself will directly intervene to destroy evil and establish righteousness, to a time when God will vindicate His people who so often are downtrodden during the present era. In contrast to general

prophecy, which puts primary emphasis on the historical setting and then moves to eschatological implications, apocalyptic tends to view history as if from the end-time itself, when history is consummated in a grand and glorious eschatological climax. In other words, whereas general prophecy looks at world history from the standpoint of man's position (or God's view of it from where man is), apocalyptic can be said to view history from the standpoint of God's position in both place and time. It has, as it were, a peculiarly transcendental focus. From the standpoint of literary device, it could be said that whereas the historical setting is primary for general prophecy, the historical setting is functional for apocalyptic.

4. *"Implied ethic."* Biblical literature in general lays great stress on ethic, but in apocalyptic literature this stress is not readily apparent. Some scholars, such as Leroy Waterman, have concluded that the prophetic line and the apocalyptic tradition are two utterly conflicting positions.[1] Recent scholarship has gone far, however, toward showing that apocalyptic is not really hate literature at all, nor even simply a psychological projection of a paradise to compensate for abject conditions suffered in this world. Rather, it is thoroughly imbued with ethical concerns. Ethic underlies all its major portrayals and is pervasive in its tone and attitude—an ethic which may be called "implied ethic" because it is not explicitly spelled out.[2]

5. *Origin in times of distress and perplexity.* Apocalyptic literature tends to arise in times of distress, perplexity, and persecution. This is true of Daniel, of Revelation, and of the non-canonical apocalypses. The type of literature which reveals God as the Master of history, and as One who will fully vindicate His people at a grand and glorious eschatological climax, is a kind of literature which is particularly suited to give comfort to oppressed and downtrodden servants of God.

6. *Basis in visions and dreams.* A comparison of apocalyptic literature with general prophecy and other Biblical literature immediately reveals that apocalyptic is characterized by much more frequent reference to visions and dreams than any other kind of literature found in the Bible.

7. *Extensive use of symbolism.* A further distinguishing feature of apocalyptic is its very extensive use of symbolism. General prophecy uses symbolism to some degree, but apocalyptic literature is thoroughly

---

[1] Waterman, *The Religion of Jesus* (New York, 1952), pp. 68-77, and *passim*.

[2] The relationship of eschatology and ethics (and apocalyptic and ethics) has been treated by Amos N. Wilder, *Eschatology and Ethics in the Teaching of Jesus* (rev. ed.; New York, 1950).

permeated with symbols of various sorts.

8. *Use of composite symbolism.* Moreover, the symbolism that is used in apocalyptic literature tends to depart often from the conventional frame of reference. For example, it makes use of pictures of animals that are non-existent in nature, such as the seven-headed dragon and beasts in Revelation 12, 13, and 17. Composite symbolism of this sort was common, however, in the art and literature of the ancient Near East.

9. *Prose literary form.* In contrast to the general prophets, who frequently use a poetic form, apocalyptic literature is normally cast into prose. Bible versions whose typography tends to distinguish between prose and poetry, such as the Revised Standard Version, make this fact clear. However, the prose nature of apocalyptic in no way destroys the symbolic character of the work. The difference is that the symbolisms tend to fall within a prose context rather than a poetic context.

The Biblical Perspective

The book of Revelation is part of Biblical literature and shares in what may be called the "Biblical perspective." Among notable features of this perspective are the following:

1. *Historical emphasis and historization.* The Bible contains a theme in which God is not only Creator of the universe but also the Arbiter of history who manifests Himself to man through His activity in history. This activity of God in history is an ongoing one, which culminates in the greatest act of history, the life and mission of Jesus Christ. The historical emphasis includes a theological recital of history (illustrated in such books as Deuteronomy, Joshua, Judges, Kings, and Chronicles, and also in the sermons of Peter and Paul in the Book of Acts) and presentation of detailed historical settings (witness the chronological items in Kings and Chronicles and also historical and chronological data in many of the Old Testament prophets). There is also a historization of symbols. Whereas, for example, in ancient pagan literature the seven-headed leviathan or *lotan* is a mythological figure representing a sea dragon or the forces of chaos, in Biblical literature this symbol is historicized. In Jewish apocalyptic there is reference in Ethiopic Enoch, in the Baruch Apocalypse, and in IV Ezra to two beasts, the seven-headed *lotan* from the sea and a beast from the earth. They are mentioned in relationship to their creation and to their becoming food in a messianic banquet. Two similar beasts are referred to in Revelation 13, but with a widely different significance: Here the

beasts are symbols of forces active in a struggle going on within history.[3]

2. *Eschatological emphasis*. Another major Bible theme is that world history is moving toward an end. It will culminate in a final act in which God will conclude it and replace it with the setting up of His eternal kingdom.

3. *The present care of God for His children*. It is important to note in Biblical literature that God is a "very present help in trouble" for His children (Ps. 46:1). In spite of many evil turns which life in this world renders them, the assurance is given that God is still in command of the currents and cross-currents of life—past, present, and future. As stated in the book of Revelation, He is the One Who was, Who is, and Who is to come (1:4).

4. *The concept of divine ethic prevailing*. Although throughout Biblical literature there are reflections of a controversy between good and evil, the assurance is given that right will prevail in the end. To some degree this is happening even in the stream of this world's history as God "removes kings and sets up kings" (Dan. 2:21) and as "righteousness exalts a nation but sin is a reproach to any people" (Prov. 14:34). But although all events are not presently in full harmony with His plan, eventually divine ethic shall prevail. The time will come when "the earth shall be full of the knowledge of the Lord, as the waters cover the sea" (Isa. 11:9).

5. *The theme of God being ever the same*. This God who watches over His people now and will give them victory in the end is ever the same in His care for them, as well as the same in His attitude toward right and wrong. What He did for His people in delivering them from old Egypt He will do again in delivering them from a symbolic new Egypt. Likewise, He who delivered them from ancient Babylon will deliver them from modern Babylon. Herein, incidentally, lies the basis for some of the symbolisms which we find in the book of Revelation.[4]

---

[3]Cf. G. E. Wright, *God Who Acts* (London, 1952), pp. 47-49; and especially Howard Wallace, "Leviathan and the Beast in Revelation," *Biblical Archaeologist*, XI (1948), 61-68. (Wallace's comment on Rev. 21:1, "and the sea was no more," as "a graphic symbol of the complete abolition of evil in the world" [p. 68] is also instructive and helps toward a realization of how pervasive symbolism is in the book of Revelation.)

[4]James D. Smart, *The Interpretation of Scripture* (Philadelphia, 1961), pp. 82, 83, has pointed out a theme of Promise and Fulfillment (rather than Prediction and Fulfillment) which is akin to what I am saying here. In this discussion,

[footnote continued]

6. *Abstraction by typical example.* It should be noted that Biblical literature in general is not philosophical. It is non-systematic in its mode of presentation. Thus it differs from "systematic theology," which represents the effort of modern theologians to make Bible truth relevant to our day in terms that are understandable to us—and thereby utilizing logical categories consistent with our current thought patterns. The Biblical perspective is characterized rather by what may be called "abstraction by typical example": No thorough-going exposition is given, but instead a principle is expounded by typical illustrations of its operation in history.

New Testament Perspective

In addition to the foregoing elements of the "Biblical perspective," mention must also be made of the New Testament emphasis on the life, death, and resurrection of Christ and on the presence of the Holy Spirit with the church. These themes are prominent in the book of Revelation as well as in other New Testament literature.

Considerations in Interpretation

In reaching a sound hermeneutic for interpretation of the book of Revelation, it is necessary to take into account the apocalyptic and Biblical perspectives mentioned above. But it is also important to consider the question of the language of this literature. That language, with its symbolisms, is part and parcel of the thought patterns and conceptual framework of the time of writing and must be recognized as such. It must be realized, as well, that whenever there is evidence of cultural borrowing, a "functional shift" tends to operate and relate the meaning of the borrowed terminology to the context of the borrowing community. Thus, the same outward expressions may signify widely different inner meaning.

The following statement on the nature of religious language is well worth noting:

[footnote continued]

which appears within a chapter on "Unity of the Bible," Smart points out (in referring to the mystery of Christ) that partial fulfillments point beyond themselves to the fulfillment yet to come. I would suggest a similar implication with respect to the use of such terms as "Babylon" in the book of Revelation: God's manifestations in the past—His great redemptive activities—will repeat themselves in greater fulfillments yet to come and of which those former experiences were, in a sense, a foretaste and promise.

The Bible points to God as its author; yet it was written by human hands; and in the varied style of its different books it presents the characteristics of the several writers. The truths revealed are all "given by inspiration of God" (2 Tim. 3:16); yet they are expressed in the words of men. The Infinite One by His Holy Spirit has shed light into the minds and hearts of His servants. He has given dreams and visions, symbols and figures; and those to whom the truth was thus revealed, have themselves embodied the thought in human language.[5]

---

[5]E. G. White, "Introduction," *The Great Controversy* (Mountain View, Calif., 1888), pp. v, vi.

CHAPTER III

SYMBOLS IN THE REVELATION

Ancient literature, like modern, makes frequent use of imagery and of figures of speech such as metaphor, simile, metonymy, synechdoche, hyperbole, and others. In some ancient literature, such as apocalyptic, there is extensive use of symbols, as we have noted earlier. The term "symbol" as used herein signifies any description which is intended to represent something other than what it normally, commonly, or usually designates or depicts.[1]

Interpreting the Symbolism of Revelation

In studying the symbolism of the book of Revelation we find that sometimes there are whole passages that are cast into a symbolic vein. At other times, where the language seems more literal, there are specific items which are symbols. Sometimes many symbols are crowded together within a short span. In order to understand and interpret properly the symbolism of the book of Revelation this symbolism must be recognized for what it is, just as is true in the case of symbolism in modern literature. The reasons for use of symbols must be understood, and then the symbols must be interpreted in relationship to both (1) their conventional meanings at the time of writing, and (2) the immediate literary context (textual setting) in which they appear.

Reasons for Using Symbols

Several reasons for use of symbols in the book of Revelation, as in other apocalyptic literature, may be pointed out:

1. *Protection.* A very important reason for use of symbols is for the sake of protecting the community using them. Messages are cast into cryptic language understood only by the members of the community itself, thus safeguarding the community against recrimination when conveying information which might endanger it.

2. *Effective illustration.* Symbol often is the most convenient or forceful way to portray a message. As is said, "A picture can replace a thousand words." Road maps and chemical formulae are examples of symbols of a certain kind, and they save many words. In apocalyptic

---

[1]In a certain sense, all words and all language are symbols, of course, but herein the common and more restricted meaning is intended.

literature, symbols are especially useful because of the cosmic sweep encompassed in this type of literature.

3. *Traditional use.* Some symbols are used simply because they are common parlance of the community using them. In other words, they have become idiomatic, as it were.

Sources of Symbolism in the Book of Revelation

In order to recognize conventional meanings of symbols, it is necessary to look for the sources of the symbolism. What are these sources for symbols in the book of Revelation? The following may be noted:

1. *Preceding Biblical literature.* As one studies the book of Revelation, he is immediately impressed with numerous reflections from such Old Testament books as Daniel, Ezekiel, Zechariah, and Jeremiah. Compare, for example, the vision of the "Ancient of days" in Daniel 7 with the vision of Christ in Revelation 1; the four beasts of Daniel 7 with the characteristics of the first beast of Revelation 13; the judgment scene of Daniel 7 with that of Revelation 20; the four living creatures and cherubim of Ezekiel 1 and 10 with the four living creatures of Revelation 4; the "four sore punishments" of Ezekiel 14 with the mission of the fourth horseman in Revelation 6; the work of marking people in Ezekiel 9 with the sealing work of Revelation 7; the horses and chariots of Zechariah 1 and 6 with the horsemen of Revelation 6; and the doom of Babylon and call out of Babylon in Jeremiah 50 and 51 with the doom of Babylon and call out of Babylon in Revelation 17, 18, and 14:8. Also, there is in the Revelation frequent allusion to the temple. Background for this is found in the Pentateuchal literature, but perhaps the temple of the writer's own day furnished the closest point of reference. The New Testament emphasis on Christ and on the Holy Spirit is evident, too, throughout the book of Revelation.

2. *The world of religious thought of the writer and hearers.* The symbolisms of two witnesses in Revelation 11 and terms such as "Egypt" in that same chapter and "Babylon" in chapters 14, 17, and 18 are items which may be classified as belonging to the world of religious thought of the writer and hearers. The dragon and beasts of chapters 12, 13, and 17 may also be considered as being in this category.

3. *Customs and practices prevailing at the time.* In the letters to the seven churches in Revelation 2 and 3 there are numerous reflections of objects, organizations, events, customs, and practices current at the time of John. Such, for example, are the gold, clothing, and eye salve of

Laodicea; the guilds of Thyatira; and other items. The merchants in Revelation 18 would be a further example. And another illustration of which more will be said in Chapters V and VI is the seven-sealed book referred to in Revelation 5.

When to Expect the Use of Symbolism

The very nature of apocalyptic indicates that we should expect frequent use of symbols in the book of Revelation. But there are places where the language seems relatively more symbolic than it does in other places. What sort of considerations should be kept in mind regarding the question of when to expect symbolism? In general, we may expect symbols to be used in direct proportion to the following:

1. *The people's vocabulary of common symbolic usage.* The terms "Egypt" and "Babylon," for example, were part of the people's vocabulary of common symbolic usage. Hence their appearance should not be surprising.

2. *Prior use of the specific symbol in the same Bible book.* Once a symbol has been introduced, it may be repeated. This is simply a matter of antecedent.

3. *The people's inability to understand items literally.* For a subject so vast as the cosmic struggle between good and evil, use of symbolic presentation should be expected. Features of this struggle could hardly be explicated literally; therefore symbols would be used to present a clearer picture of things which the hearers would have difficulty in visualizing and understanding otherwise.

4. *Portrayal of the future.* The Revelation itself claims to unveil the future.[2] But how else or how better can the future be portrayed than in symbolic terms?

5. *Desire to veil the message for the sake of protection.* Since apocalyptic emanates at a time when oppression of the community predisposes it toward a protective mode of communication, it is indeed natural to find symbols in apocalyptic literature. And within that literature the specific items which especially need to be veiled for such protective pruposes can usually be expected to be portrayed in symbol.

Understanding the Symbols in the Revelation

Knowing when to expect symbolic language, discovering the sources of the symbolism, and remembering the reasons for the use of

---

[2]Note, *e.g.,* Rev. 1:1,19; 22:6 (quoted at the beginning of Chap. V, below).

symbols—these are all important toward understanding the symbols which occur in the book of Revelation, as is also the ascertaining of conventional meanings of those symbols to John and his hearers. Essential, too, is a careful consideration of the textual settings in which the symbols are used and how they are used in those settings. Attention to such items helps toward a common-sense approach to the book of Revelation and is indeed vital as a safeguard in arriving at a rational and consistent hermeneutic. Perhaps nothing should be emphasized more strongly than the need for a sound approach which avoids the bizarre interpretations that so often arise when symbols are misunderstood, misapplied, or literalized.

Fluidity of Symbol

Symbols are picturesquely descriptive; as such they are fluid, not static, in nature. There is fluidity in the very fact that symbols can so readily creep in and out of any literary passage; but the real fluidity of symbols is different from, and more basic than, this. We may note the following aspects: (1) The same symbol may signify different things in different contexts. For example, "lion" may be used to refer to Christ (Lion of Judah, Revelation 5:5), to the devil ("roaring lion," I Peter 5:8), Judah ("lion's whelp," Genesis 49:9), and Assyria and Babylon ("the lions," Jeremiah 50:17). For proper interpretation, a conventional meaning which harmonizes with the immediate context (textual setting) is needed. (2) Different symbols may be used to represent the same thing (for example, both Lion and Lamb to represent Christ in Revelation 5). (3) A symbolic pattern may contain variation of symbols depicting the same thing within the same context (Christ as both the Shepherd and the Door into the sheepfold in John 10; the seven heads of the beast as being also "seven mountains" and "seven kings" in Revelation 17; and the "seven candlesticks" as being also "seven churches" in Revelation 1). (4) Details may vary in what are apparently the same symbols (each of the four living creatures in Ezekiel 1 has four faces whereas in Revelation 4 each one has a different face, though the descriptions of the faces are in both instances the same).

When the fluid nature of symbol is understood, variations of the kind noted above are not troublesome. Moreover, this very nature of symbol should in itself be a deterrent against over-literalness in interpretation.

Some Suggestions for Interpreting Symbols

As a matter of convenience—and as a summary of foregoing considerations—, the following list of suggestions for interpreting symbols in Revelation is given:

1. Understand the symbol for what it is: It is *symbol,* which is fluid and representative in nature.

2. Recognize the reasons for using the symbol.

3. Discover as far as possible the source or sources of the symbolism, noting both the original meaning and any derived meaning for the community now using it.

4. Consider the symbol from the standpoint of the literary type in which it occurs (*apocalyptic* for the book of Revelation, a type which is characterized by broad scope, eschatological emphasis, striking contrasts, *et cetera*).

5. Note the relationship of the symbol to the main theme that is being treated.

6. Consider the symbol within its immediate literary context or textual setting.

7. Interpret the symbol in relationship to its conventional usage or usages within the community using it, determining its precise meaning on the basis of the theme being treated and the immediate textual setting in which the symbol appears.

8. For historical application, take care not to "tailor-make" history to fit preconceived ideas of what the application of the message should be; rather let the message itself be the guide as to historical fulfillment.

9. Do not seek to find an application for every detail of an extended symbolism; instead, get the main picture or lesson. Parts of symbolic presentations are often there simply to round out the picture.

10. Recognize that the extent of a symbolic presentation may vary from a simple metaphor to an extended allegory and that the meaning of a specific symbol may vary in different contexts.

Demythologizing

The term "demythologizing" is used commonly today to represent the process by which Bible truth is extracted from an ancient world-view in order to be made meaningful in a modern context. As employed by certain scholars, it tends to reject the necessity of careful considera-tion of ancient symbolisms because these are assumed to be irrelevant to contemporary life. These symbolisms are discarded in the effort to discover the central kernel or core of truth. Actually the process is two-fold, for not only are the ancient world-view and its symbolisms rejected as a framework for the expression of Bible truth today, but that very same "Bible truth" is then re-mythologized, as it were, by putting it into the framework of our own modern world-view and its cluster of symbolisms.

There is, of course, a point of reasonableness to the approach; namely, the fact that for us today to understand religious truth, that truth must be placed within *our* frame of reference and *our* ability to understand. However, the process as it is used by both socio-historical and existentialist interpreters tends to rob the Biblical message of its original meaning. For example, when the apocalyptic language of the New Testament describing Christ's second coming and the climactic end of the age is considered to be a revelation of either the social gospel or individual Christian experience, there is good reason to question whether that language has been treated fairly.[3] In fact, we may wonder if such methodology leaves us any satisfactory criterion at all by which to tell whether we are dealing with Bible truth rather than merely our own concepts. Should we treat modern literature in this way—removing imagery and figures of speech in order to reach the core of truth—, we would undoubtedly be laughed to scorn!

A much more sensible approach has been provided by Paul Minear, who points out that the terms, symbols, and concepts of the Bible writers belong together and cannot be separated from the whole or put into a different context without losing something. The key words of these Bible writers "are the structural girders that support an entire edifice of thought. They bear not only their own weight, but a mammoth construction of assumptions, implications and affiliations."[4]

---

[3]Wilder, *op. cit.,* pp. 61-66, has given a good critique of these views.

[4]Quoted in *ibid.,* p. 66 (from an unpublished paper). In referring to critics of R. Bultmann, Wilder himself points out (*ibid.*) that only through the "mythology" or "rich symbolic expression can the fulness and wholeness of the message be conveyed and safeguarded. If in the interests of a modern scientific apologetic we are tempted to reject the pictorial vehicles we end in either rationalism or psychologism."

In a number of his published works Minear has come to grips with the questions of meaning and of relevance in relationship to ancient symbolism. One could profitably notice, for example, his remarks in his *The Kingdom and the Power: an Exposition of the New Testament Gospel* (Philadelphia, 1950), pp. 12, 13, 259, 260 (from his Preface and his note 34, respectively). Also see "Essay II" in the Appendix of the present volume.

Indeed, any methodology that summarily dismisses or radically reinterprets apocalyptic language in Biblical literature is suspect. The language—apocalyptic or otherwise—in which any Biblical message is cast is the very key by which to get to the message. Rejecting this key leaves no avenue by which to gain the meaning intended. The important thing is not to reject the symbols as relics of a by-gone age and of an outdated world-view but rather to grasp the significance of the symbols in conveying the message. In other words, we must find meaning *through* the symbols, not in spite of them or by rejecting them. It is thus, and only thus, that the relevance of the message for us may be gained.

CHAPTER IV

EXAMPLES OF LITERARY ANALYSIS OF THE REVELATION

Some pieces of literature may be thrown together in haphazard fashion. Not so the book of Revelation! Even a cursory glance at this work reveals it to be a piece of magnificent literary art, with its series of sevens and various recurring themes and symbolisms. Relatively few scholars have, however, subjected the book to as careful a literary analysis as it deserves. And yet, precisely such analysis is necessary for seeing the messages of this book in their proper relationship. It is therefore fundamental to developing a sound hermeneutic.

The next chapter will give a brief introduction to my own attempt at literary analysis of the Revelation, and the following (and final) one will seek to work out—or at least suggest—a few consequences of that attempt. It may be well first, however, to glance at some other attempts at literary analysis. Inasmuch as there is frequently a relationship between a scholar's general viewpoint toward the interpretation of the Revelation and the results of his literary analysis (we would hope more from the latter to the former than *vice versa*, though this is obviously not always the case), we classify the few analyses sampled here under the traditional futurist, continuous-historical (straight-line and recapitulationist), and preterist categories, plus "philosophy of history."

Futurist

Not much can be said regarding traditional futurist analyses of the structure of the book of Revelation, for most futurist interpreters have paid relatively little attention to the matter of careful literary analysis. However, the series of sevens—churches, seals, trumpets, plagues—are so obvious that they cannot be missed, and they form a sort of core structure for whatever rudimentary literary outline is developed by most futurists (and by many other interpreters as well). Futurist interpreters often see the seven churches as applicable to successive periods in the history of the Christian church, with the material from Revelation 4:1 onward depicting (as we noted in Chapter I) a succession of events in a still-future eschatological period.

There is one futurist interpreter who deserves special notice here because of his more than usual amount of attention to literary structure in the Revelation, as well as his balance in presentation; namely, Merrill

C. Tenney. In his book *Interpreting Revelation* (Grand Rapids, Mich., 1957), he devotes Chapter III (pp. 32-41) to this very question of literary structure and adds elsewhere other notations regarding literary features. He finds his key to the major subdivisions of the book of Revelation in certain phrases which are repeated in that book, the "first and simplest" of which phrases is "in the Spirit": "I was in the Spirit on the Lord's day," 1:10; "Straightway I was in the Spirit," 4:2; "And he carried me away in the Spirit," 17:3; and again "And he carried me away in the Spirit," 21:10 (p. 32). These phrases provide a basis, according to Tenney, for four main subdivisions of the book (aside from a Prologue and an Epilogue). Other literary facets supporting this four-fold division may be found in phrases locating the seer in different places: Patmos, 1:9; "up hither" and "a throne set in heaven," 4:1,2; wilderness, 17:3; and "a mountain great and high," 21:10. Two pairs of expressions are also linked with the same subdivisions: "a great voice," 1:10 and 4:1; and "one of the seven angels that had the seven bowls," 17:1 and 21:9 (p. 33). The subdivisions given by Tenney (excluding Prologue and Epilogue) are as follows (p. 33):

Christ in the Church	1:9–3:22
Christ in the Cosmos	4:1–16:21
Christ in Conquest	17:1–21:8
Christ in Consummation	21:9–22:5

In Tenney's opinion, the content of each of these sections is quite uniform. There are, of course, other repeated phrases in the book of Revelation, and Tenney notes some of them as contributing to further literary subdivisions within the main ones indicated above (p. 34).

All things considered, serious question may be raised as to whether Tenney has not oversimplified the literary aspects of the book of Revelation by his subdivisions and the basis upon which he has made them. His outline fits well with his futurist point of view, but has it really been extracted from the book of Revelation itself by sufficiently careful work? Or is there a danger that it is somewhat artificial?

Continuous-Historical Straight-Line

Virtually nothing can be said about the analysis of literary structure by straight-line continuous-historical interpreters of Revelation, for their tendency has been simply to ignore structure except on the most elementary level. Their interest has been mainly that of endeavoring to select events in history which might possibly be fulfillments of the prophecies of the book.

Continuous-Historical Recapitulationist

A typical continuous-historical recapitulationist interpreter is William Hendriksen, *More Than Conquerors* (Grand Rapids, Mich., 1940). He sees in the book of Revelation seven parallel themes carried through history. These seven themes he divides into two major sections. His outline may be summarized as follows (p. 30):[1]

    I. The Struggle on Earth (the Church Persecuted, Avenged, Protected, Victorious)

        1. Christ Among 7 Lampstands, chaps. 1–3
        2. 7–Sealed Book, chaps. 4–7
        3. 7 Trumpets, chaps. 8–11

    II. The Deeper Spiritual Background (Christ and the Church Persecuted by the Dragon and His Helpers, and Then Victorious)

        4. The Woman and Child Persecuted by the Dragon and His Helpers, chaps. 12–14
        5. 7 Bowls of Wrath, chaps. 15, 16
        6. Fall of the Harlot and Beasts, chaps. 17–19
        7. Judgment on Satan; and Then the New Heaven, New Earth, New Jerusalem, chaps. 20–22

Hendriksen points out that each of the seven lines of prophecy takes us down the stream of history toward the eschatological climax, each line taking us further into eschatology and revealing the "Great Consummation" more fully (the final one takes us, of course, to the New Heaven, New Earth, and New Jerusalem). The progressive parallelism may be diagrammed as follows (a more detailed diagram appears on p. 48 of his book):

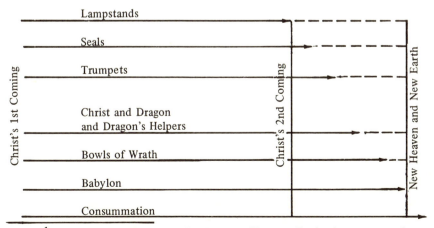

[1]The various outlines in this chapter will normally be in summary form rather than precisely as given in the original publications.

From a certain point of view, Hendriksen may be considered more of a "philosophy-of-history" interpreter than a purely continuous-historical recapitulationist. However, an interpreter who is clearly and definitely a continuous-historical recapitulationist is Uriah Smith, *Thoughts on Daniel and the Revelation* (rev. ed.; Nashville, Tenn., 1944). Smith sees specific fulfillments for the various items in different parallel lines of prophecy in Revelation. He has not, however, given attention to the literary structure of the book as such.   His work, like that of Hendriksen, is based largely on the more apparent surface features (the series of sevens, *et cetera*). He finds the churches, seals, trumpets, and the dragon and beasts of Revelation 12 and 13 as representing different aspects of church history from the apostolic era to the second coming of Christ. The plagues of chapter 16 are considered entirely eschatological or future, but chapters 17 and 18 go back more or less into historical ground. Finally, chapters 19-22 relate once again to the eschatological future.

Preterist

As an example of a preterist outline of literary structure of the book of Revelation, I present in summary form that of Thomas S. Kepler, *The Book of Revelation* (New York, 1957), pp. 35-40, but omitting the Prologue and Epilogue. Kepler finds 7 "visions" and 10 "scenes" as follows:

1. Son of God in the Church, 1:9–3:22

    (1) Setting for the Vision, 1:9–20
    (2) Letters to the 7 Churches, 2:1–3:22

2. God's Plan for History, 4:1–8:1

    (3) The Court of Heaven, 4:1–5:14
    (4) Opening the 7 Seals, 6:1–8:1
    (including Chap. 7 as a parenthesis)

3. Church Faces Trouble, 8:2–11:19

    (5) The 7 Trumpets, 8:7–11:19
    (Including 10:1–11:13 as a parenthesis)

4. Battle and Victory, 12:1–14:20

    (6) Parenthesis: Oracles About the Last Judgment, 12:1–14:20

5. God's Wrath, 15:1–16:21

    (7) The 7 Last Plagues, 15:1–16:21

6.   Babylon Judged, 17:1–20:10

    (8)   Fall of Harlot Babylon, 17:1–18:24
    (9)   Return of Victorious Christ, 19:1–20:10

7.   God's Purpose Consummated in New Jersualem, 20:11–22:5

    (10)   Vision of End of World and of New Jerusalem, 20:11–22:5

Analyses providing a basic sevenfold division of the Apocalypse have been developed by a number of other scholars, including Ernst Lohmeyer, *Die Offenbarung des Johannes* (Tübingen, 1926) and John Wick Bowman, *The Drama of the Book of Revelation* (Philadelphia, 1955) and *Interpreter's Dictionary of the Bible* (1962), 4: 64-65. Bowman refers to his major divisions as "acts" and divides *each* of these 7 "acts" into 7 "scenes"– thus arriving at a total of 49 "scenes," whereas Kepler has found only 10. It should be further noted that whereas both Kepler and Bowman deal with almost the entire book of Revelation (1:9-22:5) in outlining their 7 major divisions, Lohmeyer finds his in a somewhat smaller portion of the Revelation (6:1-21:4), which he calls the "Apocalyptic Part." Each of his main divisions he subdivides into 7 "visions." For the sake of convenient overview, a summary of the 7 main divisions of Lohmeyer's and Bowman's outlines are placed in parallel columns below.

Ernst Lohmeyer	*J. W. Bowman*
1. The 7 Seal Visions, 6:1-8:1	1. The Church on Earth, 1:9-3:22
2. The 7 Trumpet Visions, 8:2-11:15	2. God's Purpose in History, 4:1-8:1
3. The 7 Visions of the Kingdom of the Dragon, 11:15-13:18	3. The Church in Tribulation, 8:2-11:18
4. The 7 Visions of the Coming of the Son of Man, 14:1-20	4. The Salvation of the Church, 11:19-15:4
5. The 7 Bowl Visions, 15:1-16:21	5. The World in Agony, 15:5-16:21
6. The 7 Visions of the Fall of Babylon, 17:1-19:10	6. The Judgment of the World, 17:1-20:3
7. The 7 Visions of the Consummation, 19:11-21:4	7. The Church in the Millennium, 20:4-22:5

Both Lohmeyer and Bowman have focused on what may be termed a "dramatic" view of the Revelation. The former has done so from virtually an "ahistorical" perspective, whereas the latter's preterist stance is more evident.

A rather recent example of an outline which itself highlights a preterist stance has been provided by Wilfrid J. Harrington, O.P., *Understanding the Apocalypse* (Washington, D.C., 1969), pp. 25-28. The three major divisions of this outline are as follows:

1. The Church and Israel, 4:1–11:19
2. The Church and Pagan Rome, 12:1–20:15
3. The New Jerusalem, 21:1–22:5

Philosophy of History

Although the individuals mentioned in the immediately preceding section have been classified as "preterist," it should be kept in mind that they may also have some leanings toward what we have called "philosophy of history." We now come, however, to two individuals whose leanings in this direction are sufficiently strong that we may classify them as "philosophy-of-history" interpreters: D. T. Niles and Paul S. Minear.

In his book *As Seeing the Invisible* (New York, 1961), Niles has analyzed and treated the contents of the Revelation in such a way that the following outline would summarize the literary structure he has found, aside from introductory and concluding sections (pp. 37, 101-106):

I. The Lord and His Church: The Unveiling of God's Person, 1:12–3:22

    1a. Opening Vision, 1:12–18;
    1b. Letters to the Churches, 2:1–3:22
        (1)–(4) 4 Churches Tempted to Compromise
        (5) Sardis
        (6) Philadelphia
        (7) Laodicea

II. The Lord and His World: The Unveiling of God's Purpose, 4:1–11:19

    2a. Throne in Heaven, 4:1–5:14;
    2b. Judgment and Mercy, 6:1–8:1
        (1)–(4) 4 Horsemen: Loss of Peace
        (5) Earthquake: Loss of Stability
        (6) Sealed Multitude
        (7) Unsealed Scroll

    3a. Altar in Heaven, 8:2–5;
    3b. Wages of Sin, and Gift of Kingdom, 8:6–11:19
        (1)–(4) 4 Trumpets: Loss of Subsistence
        (5) Woes: Loss of Faith
        (6) Gospel
        (7) Kingdom Comes

III. The Lord of All Rule: The Unveiling of God's Power, 12:1–22:5

    4a. God's Purpose in Travail, 12:1–17;
    4b. Christ *Imperator*, 13:1–14:20
        (1)–(4) 4 Monsters: The Rebellion of Evil
        (5) Mark of Beast and of Lamb
        (6) Nature of Judgment
        (7) Close of an Age

    5a. Song of Salvation, 15:1–8;
    5b. Christ *Victor*, 16:1–19:4
        (1)–(4) 4 Plagues: Beginning of the End
        (5) The Last Issue
        (6) Judgment Executed
        (7) Babylon is No More

    6a. Great Hallelujah, 19:5–16;
    6b. Christ *Pantokrator*, 19:17–22:21 (22:5)
        (1)–(4) 4 Powers: End of Their Misrule
        (5) The Final Encounter
        (6) The Last Judgment
        (7) The Eternal City

Although Niles himself does not combine his materials into precisely the foregoing pattern, a combination of these materials does reveal that the above outline represents fairly his views. He points out (p. 105) that the book of Revelation consists of "six movements" spread into its three major sections, and that each movement "begins with a Christophany and proceeds through seven events." The units of seven are simply John's raw materials, however; they are not the determinant for his basic pattern of arrangement. The principles on which the structure of the book is designed, according to Niles, are principles pertaining to the realms of history and liturgy (p. 106). He then proceeds to analyze the literary pattern of the book on the basis of the weekly sequence, festal year, and daily liturgy (pp. 106-114), following up the discussion with a summarizing chart (p. 115).

Though we cannot here take space to analyze Niles' material on liturgy, I would point out that it makes very intriguing reading. Question may be raised, of course, as to its validity. So also is the case with the outline given above, which is related to it. That outline appears in some ways to be more the concept of the modern writer than the natural pattern of the original book itself. The idea of seven events consistently pushed into a "(1)-(4), (5), (6), (7)" arrangement may fit liturgy, but surely seems artificial in some instances as far as the content of the book of Revelation is concerned. Moreover, why has the 5th seal been omitted entirely? And why do the 7 churches represent the 7 events of that movement, whereas the seals and trumpets spread into only 6 events of their respective movements, and the plagues into only 5 events of its movement?

As we turn to Paul S. Minear's recent book *I Saw a New Earth* (Washington, D.C., 1968), we come to what is undoubtedly one of the most careful literary analyses of the book of Revelation to have appeared in print. Minear divides the Revelation into sections, providing in each section (1) his own translation of the text in a typographical arrangement which gives prominence to literary features and (2) a discussion of the literary structure of the section. Unfortunately, he does not give similar careful discussion of the overall outline of the book, but that outline may be ascertained nonetheless from various chapter titles. Aside from the Introduction and Conclusion, it would be as follows:

1. Promise of Victory, 1:9–3:22
2. Lamb as Victor, 4:1–8:1
3. The Prophets as Victors, 8:2–11:18
4. The Faithful as Victors, 11:19–15:4
5. Victory over Babylon, 15:5–19:10
6. Victory over the Devil, 19:11–22:7

It will be noted that Minear's outline gives prominence to the theme of victory.

Although I differ from Minear in a number of matters of interpretation (as does even the writer of the Foreword to his book, Myles M. Bourke), I most heartily commend the effort Minear has put into literary analysis, an item which is so often neglected although it has a vital connection with hermeneutics.[2]

Further Efforts at Literary Analysis

Even though many interpreters of the Revelation have done very little toward analyzing the literary structure of the book, the foregoing outlines by no means exhaust the illustrations that are available from scholars who have made serious attempts at analysis. Nor do those outlines represent all the possible variations of outlook toward the Apocalypse. Some further analyses, which especially bring to view elements not thus far touched upon, will be called to attention in Essay III in the Appendix to the present volume.

---

[2]See "Essay II" in the Appendix of the present volume for further information regarding Minear's contributions, including a review of his *I Saw a New Earth.*

Factors Involved in Adequate Literary Analysis

A multiplicity of factors is obviously involved in adequate literary analysis of the Apocalypse, and the amount of attention or inattention given to such factors leads to quite differing results, as has been aptly illustrated by the outlines presented above. Some scholars have quite evidently ignored many of the internal literary features, noting hardly anything more than the four obvious septets, whereas other scholars have perhaps gone to an opposite extreme in overly subdividing the book. Moreover, some scholars have apparently been guided quite largely by their basic interpretational approach to the Revelation, whether futurist, continuous-historical, preterist, or "philosophy of history." Perhaps no interpreter can, or even should, be so thoroughly "objective" as to make himself wholly devoid of any attitude toward the book of Revelation before undertaking a detailed literary analysis of it. However, he should always be careful to let the book speak for itself, rather than himself trying to speak for it.

For proper hermeneutic, due regard must be given to the historical setting of the book, conventional meanings of the symbolisms used in the book, nature of apocalyptic literature, the "Biblical perspective," and parallel and contrasting literary features within the book, as well as the more obvious pattern of "sevens." It is necessary also to keep in mind the purpose and the theme of the entire work as well as the main topic of each subdivision, items to which we will next turn our attention.

CHAPTER V

A NEW LITERARY ANALYSIS

This chapter will provide an outline of the Revelation based on literary analysis; but inasmuch as the purpose and theme of the Revelation pervade the whole book, and must not be ignored in literary analysis, it will be well first to note the book's own statement of these items.

Purpose

Revelation 1:1 indicates clearly the purpose of the book: "The Revelation of Jesus Christ, which God gave to Him, to show to His servants things which must shortly come to pass...." This thought is also given in the concluding section of the book, in 22:6: "The Lord God of the holy prophets sent His angel to show to His servants the things which must shortly be done." And it is noted in 1:19 as well: "Write the things which you have seen, and the things which are, and the things which shall be hereafter."

Theme

The theme of the book appears to be twofold: the promise of Christ's coming in victory at the eschatological climax, and an assurance of God's presence even now. This double theme pervades the messages throughout the book, but it is also explicitly stated in both the introductory and concluding sections of the work: Revelation 1:7,8, "Behold, He comes with clouds; and every eye shall see Him, and they also which pierced Him.... I am Alpha and Omega, the beginning and the ending, says the Lord, who is, and who was, and who is to come, the Almighty"; 22:12,13, "And, behold, I come quickly.... I am Alpha and Omega, the beginning and the end, the first and the last." Elsewhere, Christ gives the assurance that He is the One who "lives, was dead, but behold, am alive forevermore," the One who has the keys of hades and of death (1:18).

What a grand theme for a glorious book! What wonderful assurance is given to oppressed and downtrodden Christians as they learn that in their darkest hours the connection between God and His people is close and decided! What comfort there is for them to know that their Lord is with them even now, no matter how difficult their trials may be! What hope they can gain by recognizing that one day in God's own purpose He shall for His people set aright a topsy-turvy world, as Christ comes quickly to "give every man according as His work shall be" (22:12)! No wonder that John in longing anticipation exclaimed, as many Christians have echoed since, "Even so, come, Lord Jesus" (22:20).

Parallel Sections in Revelation

As the book of Revelation is read, it is virtually impossible to fail to note that there are many repetitions of symbolisms and apparently even of broader themes. For example, a "bottomless pit" is referred to in both chapters 9 and 20; the twenty-four elders and four living creatures in chapters 4 and 19; the declaration of Babylon's fall in chapters 14 and 18; the sea of glass in chapters 4 and 15; and the seven angels with the seven last plagues in chapters 15-16, 17, and 21. Some of these repetitions of symbolisms are quite random, for the symbols may be repeated simply on the basis of the rule of antecedent noted in Chapter III. Every repeated symbol undoubtedly has some meaning related to a previous appearance of the same symbol, but undue attention to repetitions on this basis may tend to disguise a more significant repetition which occurs in *broader patterns* between earlier and later portions of the book. The similarity of the trumpets to the plagues, for example, has frequently been noted, as has also certain similarities of the dragon and first beast in chapters 12, 13, with the beast in chapter 17. Here there are parallels not only of individual symbols but of sequences or major themes.

Can such parallels of sequences or major themes be discovered beyond the ones just noted? Is there perhaps a whole pattern which shows correlation between sections in a first part of the book and sections in the last part? I would suggest that a careful analysis of the book reveals that this is indeed the case. I must admit, however, that it is very difficult at times to know at just which verse to find the transition from one major section to another, and therefore the subdivisions given in the following analysis are subject to revision. But for working purposes, let us proceed with comparisons of the early portion of the Revelation with the later chapters.

Prologue and Epilogue

I have already called attention to the fact that the statements of purpose and theme in the Revelation occur both in the introductory and concluding sections of the book, which sections we may call Prologue and Epilogue. The parallels between these sections do not stop here, however. The following list provides a synopsis of these and certain other parallels found in 1:1-11 as compared with 22:6-21:

1:1	Revelation of Christ, sent by angel; "things which must shortly come to pass";
22:6	Angel sent to show "things which must shortly be done."
1:3	Blessing on those who heed;
22:7	Blessing on those who heed;
22:18,19	Warning to those who do not heed, who add or subtract.
1:4−6	Greeting to the Churches;
22:16	Exhortation and testimony to the Churches.
1:7,8	"Behold, he comes"; Alpha and Omega;
22:12,13	"Behold, I come quickly"; Alpha and Omega.
1:9,10	Opening Setting;
22:8	Concluding Setting.

It will be noted that the parallels occur largely, but not entirely, in *reverse* sequence.

The Church

The first main section of the book of Revelation (1:12-3:22) presents letters to the seven churches; these letters give a description of what may be called the "Church Militant." The last main section of Revelation (21:5-22:5) gives a description of the New Jerusalem and conditions of what may be called the "Church Triumphant." Thus the earlier section may be called *historical;* and the later one, *eschatological.* There is relationship of theme, though not in detailed literary structure. However, a number of parallel items may be noted, such as the following:

Church Militant		Church Triumphant
1:16	brightness of Christ	21:23
1:17;2:8	first & last (Alpha & Omega)	21:6
2:7	tree of life	22:2
3:5	book of life	21:27
2:11	second death	21:8
3:12	New Jerusalem	21:10
3:12	God's name written on His people	22:4
3:21	throne	22:3
3:14	faithful and true	21:5
2:7,11,17,26; 3:5,12,21	reference to overcomers	21:7

The Work for Man's Salvation

The next two main sections of the Revelation in sequence from the beginning and end, respectively, are 4:1-8:1 and 19:1-21:4. A careful reading of these two sections reveals that the earlier one treats a situation in *history,* whereas the later one deals with the era of *judgment.* Note, for example, the cry of the saints in 6:10, "How long, O Lord, . . do You not judge and avenge our blood . . ?," as compared with the announcement in 19:2, "He has judged the great harlot . . . and has avenged the blood of His servants at her hand." The nature of these two sections indicates work for man's salvation and the completion of that work.[1] Again, there is obvious similarity in theme and even in scene, though not in detailed sequence of the presentation. Among the more significant parallels, the following may be noted:

Work Progressing		Work Completed
4:2	throne	19:4; 20:11
4:4	24 elders	19:4
4:6	4 living creatures	19:4
4:9–11; 5:8–10	praise given by 4 living creatures and 24 elders	19:4
5:13	every creature (much people) giving praise	19:1,6
5:6; 7:10,17	the Lamb	19:7,9
6:2	rider on white horse	19:11
6:4	sword	19:15,21
6:10	judging and avenging	19:2
6:15	distress of great men, kings, etc.	19:17,18
7:9; 6:11	white raiment	19:8
7:9,10	multitude sings praise to God	19:6,7
7:15	God dwelling with His people	21:3
7:15	temple or tabernacle with men	21:3
7:17	tears wiped away	21:4

God's Treatment of the Wayward and Judgment on Evil Forces

The sets of paralleling sections that occur in reverse order in the book of Revelation conclude with a double series—8:2-14:20 and 15:1-18:24—having an "Exodus from Egypt"/"Fall of Babylon" motif (both the trumpets and plagues septets are reminiscent of the plagues on ancient Egypt, but merge into the Babylon theme with mention of the "great river Euphrates" in 9:14 and 16:12, respectively). The basic subsections of this series have, again, historical and eschatological counterparts:

Trumpet Warnings, 8:2–11:18;	Plague Punishments, 15:1–16:17;
Struggle with Babylon, 11:19–14:20	Judgment on Babylon, 16:18–18:24;

---

[1]More details in this regard will be furnished in Chap. VI.

Let us note some of the parallels between the trumpets and the plagues. Central items of each are as follows:

Trumpets		Plagues
8:7	earth	16:2
8:8	sea	16:3
8:10	rivers and fountains	16:4
8:12	heavenly bodies; sun	16:8
9:2	darkness	16:10
9:14	Euphrates	16:12
11:15	announcement of Christ's rule; "it is done"	16:17

Moving from the trumpets and plagues to the struggle and judgment scenes, we find such parallels as these:

Struggle		Judgment
11:19	voices, thunderings, lightnings, earthquake, and great hail	16:18,21
12:1	woman clothed with sun *versus* harlot	17:1
12:3; 13:1	animal with 7 heads & 10 horns	17:3
14:8	Babylon is fallen	18:2

Overview of Main Subdivisions; Use of Chiastic Structure

It seems more than coincidental that such parallelisms in theme should occur—and that they should occur in a generally reverse order! A reading of the main sections noted above leaves also an impression that the earlier sections in the book relate to a historical frame of reference, whereas the later sections are eschatological correlatives to the earlier ones.

This use of *chiasmus,* or inverse parallelism, may be summarized as follows (the prologue and epilogue, which also parallel each other, are omitted):

Overview of the Chiastic Structure of the Book of Revelation

Part I: Historical	Part II: Eschatological
1. Church Militant ———————————————————	6. Church Triumphant
2. God Works for Man's Salvation —————————	5. God Completes His Work for Man's Salvation
3a. Warnings to the Wayward ————————	4a. Punishment to the Wicked;
3b. Struggle with Evil Forces ————————	4b. Judgment on Evil Forces

The main reason for identifying the subdivisions by the terminology here chosen is that the basic symbolisms and content of those subdivisions indicate the subjects designated. The seven-sealed book, for example, was a will or testament, and the breaking of the seals was preliminary to the opening of the will and disclosing who would inherit and who would not. In this setting in Revelation, the breaking of the seals would therefore represent successive steps or means by which God through Christ acts in preparing the world for judgment; hence the caption, "God Works for Man's Salvation."[2] The trumpet blast was a signal of warning; hence the designation for the trumpets of "Warnings to the Wayward." And the contents of chapters 12, 13 make self-evident the reason for the choice of the term "Struggle."

Structure of Some of the Subdivisions

It may be of interest to analyze the structure of some of the main subdivisions and their subsections. In the series of seals and trumpets, and in the section dealing with the struggle between God's forces and the forces of evil (4:1-14:20), a general pattern may be seen, as follows:

God Works for Man's Salvation, 4:1–8:1
   1. Victorious Vision: Throne Room of Heaven; Lamb Worthy to
                      Open the Book, 4:1–5:14
   2. First 6 Seals, 6:1–17
   3. Spotlight on Last Events: Sealing Work; Great Multitude, 7:1–17
   4. Glorious Climax: 7th Seal, 8:1

Warnings to the Wayward, 8:2–11:18
   1. Victorious Vision: Incense Mingled with Prayer of Saints, 8:2–5
   2. First 6 Trumpets, 8:7–9:21
   3. Spotlight on Last Events: Angel and Scroll; Temple and Two
                      Witnesses, 10:1–11:14
   4. Glorious Climax: 7th Trumpet, 11:15–18

Struggle, 11:19–14:20
   1. Victorious Vision: Open Temple, and Ark, 11:19
   2. Evil Forces Attack God's People, 12:1–13:18
   3. Spotlight on Last Events: Redeemed 144,000; 3 Angels' Messages,
                      14:1–12
   4. Glorious Climax: Harvest of Earth, 14:14–20

The symmetry of the foregoing is immediately obvious, with historical series proceeding in regular fashion to an "eschatological

---

[2]More details in this regard will be furnished in Chap. VI.

climax." Even the so-called parentheses (which we have termed "Spot-light on Last Events") are in each case bipartite.

Evidences of Recapitulation

The symmetry of structure just noticed as occurring in various sections in the first main part of the book of Revelation indicates a pattern of recapitulationary sequences. The same historical ground is traversed several times, as it were, from different perspectives, with each sequence culminating in an eschatological climax.

It is interesting to note that the second major part of the book also contains evidences of recapitulation. For example, the judgmental scene of chapter 17 describing a harlot riding on a beast in the wilderness explicates, or elaborates on, the 6th and 7th plagues of the immediately preceding section, as is clear from the opening announcement in chapter 17 as well as from the reference in 17:15 to the waters upon which the harlot sits (cf. 16:12). Again, the portrayal in chapter 20 of Satan in the "bottomless pit" or "abyss" for a thousand years, of his release and revived activity thereafter, and of the final destruction befalling him and his armies fur-nishes a sort of recapitulation of (or parallel to) the description in chapter 17 relating to the beast's being in the "bottomless pit" or "abyss," its coming forth to renewed activity under an 8th head, and its finally going into perdition (vss. 8,11).

An Outline of the Book of Revelation

Based on considerations brought to attention in the present chapter, we can now pull together the various threads of discussion to formulate a tentative outline of the whole book of Revelation. This is given on page 51, below.

It is possible to make the chiastic structure stand out even more clearly by presenting the main contents of the outline in a diagrammatic sketch. Such a sketch (with necessarily abbreviated description of contents) appears on page 52.

Some Concluding Observations on Literary Analysis

In concluding this chapter, I should reiterate that the structure of the "Outline" here presented is based on a literary analysis which takes note of parallel themes and scenes rather than of parallelism in only in-dividual symbols or of mere similarities in phrasing. There is a movement from one picture to another: from the "Church Militant," to "God Works for Man's Salvation," to "God's Warnings to the Wayward and Struggle with the Forces of Evil." This is followed by another series of pictures in a movement from "God's Punishment of the Wicked and Judgment of the Forces of Evil," to "God Completes His Work for Man's Salvation," to the "Church Triumphant."

Such movements and the descriptions of major themes and scenes do not, however, obscure the fact that there is also another type of progression in the book: New symbolisms and scenes provide the setting or basis for further use of such symbolisms and scenes in later main subdivisions of the book irrespective of the parallel historical and eschatological series we have noted. This is particularly true in the eschatological section, where, for example, the judgments on Babylon in chapters 17 and 18 provide a setting for chapter 19, even though chapter 19 appears to cover again ground which is prior to some of the developments portrayed in chapter 17. Another example is the reference to one of the angels having the seven bowls of wrath in both chapter 17 and chapter 21, after these angels have been first introduced in chapters 15 and 16.

It should be emphasized that although the book of Revelation falls into two main parts, we must not expect every individual item in the first part to be historical and every individual item in the last part to be eschatological. Indeed, although the various series in the first main part of the book deal with the historical sphere, they generally move to an eschatological climax; and on the other hand, although the point of view in the last main part of the book is that of eschatology, certain items found therein involve prior history. For example, in the historical series, the seventh seal, the seventh trumpet, and the harvest of Revelation 14 are eschatological. And in the eschatological series, the appeal to "watch" in chapter 16 and the cry to "come out" of Babylon in chapter 18, as well as certain explanations of the heads of the beast in chapter 17, are from the viewpoint of history even though the basic settings are eschatological.

TENTATIVE OUTLINE OF
THE BOOK OF REVELATION

PROLOGUE (1:1–11)

   Revelation of Christ, sent by angel; "things which must shortly come to pass" (1:1)
   Blessing on those who heed (1:3)
   Greeting to the Churches (1:4–6); Two-fold theme (1:7,8); Opening setting (1:9,10)

I   *HISTORICAL SERIES* (1:12–14:20)

   1. *The Church Militant*—Counsels to God's people (1:12–3:22)

      (1) Victorious Vision
      (2) 7 Letters

   2. Conflict of the Ages in Progress (4:1–14:20)

      (1) *God Works for Man's Salvation* (4:1–8:1)
          -1- Victorious Vision—Throne room of Heaven; Lamb worthy to open Book
          -2- First 6 Seals
          -3- Spotlight on Last Events—Sealing Work; Great Multitude
          -4- Glorious Climax—7th Seal

      (2) God Warns the Wayward and Battles the Forces of Evil (8:2–11:18; 11:19–14:20)

          Warnings to the Wayward:
          -1- Victorious Vision—Incense mingled with prayers of saints
          -2- First 6 Trumpets
          -3- Spotlight on Last Events—Angel and Scroll; Temple & 2 Witnesses
          -4- Glorious Climax—7th Trumpet

          The Struggle:
          -1- Victorious Vision: Open Temple, and Ark
          -2- Evil Forces Attack God's People—Dragon & 2 Beasts
          -3- Spotlight on Last Events—144,000 with Lamb on Mt. Zion; 3 Angels' Messages
          -4- Glorious Climax—Harvest of Earth

      II. *ESCHATOLOGICAL SERIES* (15:1–22:5)

         1. Conflict of the Ages Consummated (15:1–21:4)

            (1) God Punishes the Wicked and Judges the Forces of Evil (chs. 15–18)
                Punishment to the Wicked–7 Last Plagues
                Judgment—Babylon judged

            (2) *God Completes His Work for Man's Salvation:* Christ's Advent, the 2 Suppers, the Millennium, Final Judgment, Destruction of the Wicked, New Heavens and New Earth (19:1–21:4)

         2. *The Church Triumphant*—Reward for God's people (21:5–22:5)

EPILOGUE (22:6–21)

   Angel sent to show "things which must shortly be done" (22:6)
   Blessing on those who heed (22:7)
   Concluding setting (22:8); Two-fold theme (22:12,13); Exhortation & testimony to the
       Churches (22:16); Warning to those who do not heed, who add or subtract (22:18,19)
   Closing Words (22:20,21)

CHIASTIC STRUCTURE OF THE BOOK OF REVELATION

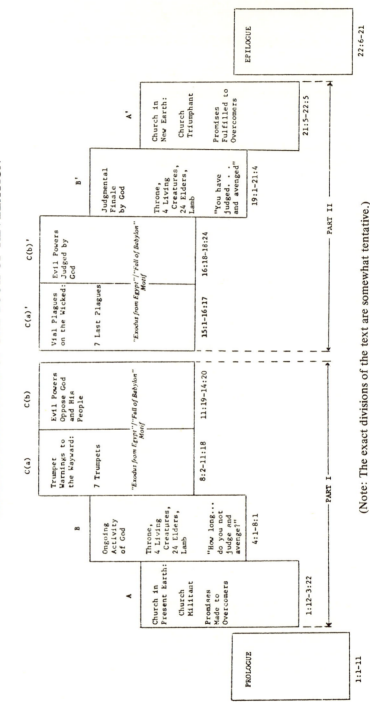

(Note: The exact divisions of the text are somewhat tentative.)

CHAPTER VI

SUGGESTIONS FOR INTERPRETATION

The literary analysis provided in the preceding chapter leads to some important hermeneutical considerations which deserve at least brief mention. The present chapter will first note these considerations and will then illustrate some implications of the analysis by means of two examples: (1) the seven-headed dragon and beasts of Revelation 12, 13, and 17; and (2) the seven-sealed book and seals of chapters 5, 6, 8:1.

Hermeneutical Considerations from the New Literary Analysis

It should be stated at the outset that although the basic chiastic structure of the book of Revelation, as outlined in Chapter V above, has an important bearing on interpretation, this fact in no way obviates the need for careful attention to various matters treated in earlier chapters (especially Chapters II and III). Thus, the hermeneutical guidelines indicated below are to be taken into account in addition to, not exclusion of, those mentioned earlier.

A basic interpretational consideration which derives from the chiastic structure of the Apocalypse is the importance of observing in which of the two major parts of the entire book any particular item appears—whether the historical or the eschatological (or in prologue or epilogue, if such be the case). Moreover, two cautions arise as corollaries: First, care must be taken to avoid any methodology which would make the messages of Revelation either entirely historical or entirely eschatological, for such would do violence to the book's division into major historical and eschatological parts. Second, it would likewise be inappropriate to adopt a system of interpretation which would set forth the messages of the Apocalypse as if they portrayed an absolutely "straightline" or completely sequential chain of events or developments. This caution applies regardless of any particular interpretational stance taken, whether preterist, continuous historical, futurist, or "philosophy of history." It likewise applies irrespective of whether the interpreter looks upon the orientation of the Apocalypse as historical, as eschatological, as dramatical, as symbolical, or as any combination of these.

A second basic hermeneutical consideration which derives from the literary analysis provided in the preceding chapter is that in interpreting the Revelation there is need to recognize the book's recapitulationary sequences. This consideration would also constitute a further caution against any methodology which attempts to interpret the book's messages according to a strictly or even primarily "straight-line" pattern.

Finally, it must not be overlooked that the very division of the book into two main parts with paralleling subsections can prove helpful as a guide towards proper interpretation of specific passages. For whenever a passage in one main part of the Revelation is understood, it can provide clues towards the meaning of the correlative passage in the other main part of the book. In following up such clues one must, of course, keep constantly in mind the frame of reference of the major part of the Revelation in which each passage occurs—whether it is the historical or the eschatological.

With the foregoing considerations in mind, together with those brought to attention in earlier chapters, we are now ready to proceed to the two examples of how some of the consequences of our literary analysis may be worked out. It should be noted that interpretation as such will not be given; rather, attention is directed to hermeneutical concerns.

The Dragon and Beasts of Revelation 12, 13, 17

In Revelation 17, a beast is described which has seven heads and ten horns and is called the "beast that was, is not, and yet is," and the beast that "is not" and "shall ascend out of the bottomless pit and go into perdition [final destruction]" (verse 8). Parallels to this beast are found in the dragon with seven heads and ten horns in chapter 12 and the beast with seven heads and ten horns in chapter 13. In each of these chapters the theme of *struggle* is prominent; but it is important to note that the first two chapters belong to a series or subdivision in Revelation which is historical, whereas chapter 17 is found in the eschatological part of the book. The context in each case reveals this very fact of *history* for chapters 12, 13, and *eschatology* for chapter 17; for the people of God are persecuted at the hands of the powers of evil in the first two chapters, whereas chapter 17 portrays judgment on the forces of evil. The presence or absence of crowns (the sign of regal power) in various of these chapters is significant too: in chapter 12, crowns are on the heads; in chapter 13, crowns are on the horns; and in chapter 17, no crowns are mentioned. For interpretational purposes, treatment of these various animals as within the scope of either the historical series or the eschatological series— whichever is appropriate—is vital. To seek a fulfillment in history, for example, for the "is not" phase of the beast of chapter 17, when that phase is obviously a view of judgment, is illogical. Or to treat the whole of chapter 17 as having historical, rather than eschatological, fulfillment is to miss the very point of the chapter and of the whole second part of the book of Revelation in which it occurs.

This is not to say, however, that there are absolutely no historical reflections in chapter 17. The explanation of the seven heads and ten horns, for example, must be from the viewpoint of John at the time of his writing. After all, how else can *explanation* be given than in terms of what exists, even though the vision itself is from the perspective of eschatological judgment when the beast *"is not"*? In other words, though John sees the vision from the "is not" phase (judgment), the heads and horns are historical entities belonging to the "was" phase.

The diagram on page 56 illustrates the concepts underlying the details regarding the beast of chapter 17.

For further amplification of the meaning of the "is not" and "yet is" phases of the beast's existence and of the statement that he ascends out of the bottomless pit and goes into perdition, a study of Revelation 20 will be instructive (see page 49 above).

The Seven-Sealed Book and Breaking of the Seals

In Revelation 5, the center of attention is a seven-sealed book or scroll which no man can open. So vital is the opening of this scroll that John weeps because no man can open it. But he is comforted to learn that the Lion of the tribe of Judah (Christ) will be able to break the seals and open the scroll. Then he sees a Lamb (an alternative symbol for Christ) come forth, take the scroll, and break the seals.

The context (chapters 4 and 5) reveals the setting to be the throne-room of heaven. Certain main symbolisms parallel similar ones in Ezekiel (the four living creatures of Ezekiel 1, for example). The central item, the seven-sealed scroll, portrays a will or testament, for that is precisely what such a seven-sealed document was in Roman law of John's day. We find, then, that the picture we have in the subdivision of Revelation from 4:1 to 8:1 is a court scene in which a will or testament is to be opened. In the context of Revelation, this will or testament would be a title-deed, as it were, to man's lost inheritance—an inheritance which has been repurchased by Christ, the Lamb. Thus the scroll is a *book of destiny*. The opening of it means inheritance in God's kingdom; its remaining closed means forfeiture. No wonder that John wept when he thought no one could open the scroll!

But the scroll is to be opened—by the Lamb, the Redeemer of man's lost inheritance. And in anticipation, songs of praise usher forth to the Lamb (5:8-14). As the Lamb opens the seals one by one (in chapter 6 and 8:1), a series of events occur. First, four horsemen go forth, reminiscent of the horsemen and chariots of Zechariah 1 and 6—God's agencies: "These are the four spirits of the heavens that go forth from standing

THE BEAST OF REVELATION 17

HISTORICAL ERA

7 Heads—Successive

1	2	3	4	5	6 John's Time	7 10 Horns Concurrent

"Five Are Fallen"   "WAS"   "One Is"   "One Is Not Yet Come"

ESCHATOLOGICAL ERA

From Bottomless Pit to Perdition →

"Bottomless Pit"	8th Head	"Perdition"

"IS NOT"   "YET IS"

before the Lord of all the earth" and who patrol the earth (see Zechariah 6:5,7). Then follow souls under the altar in the fifth seal, signs in earth and heaven in the sixth seal, and silence in heaven for half an hour in the seventh seal.

It is important to note that this whole subdivision of the Revelation is set within the *historical* rather than eschatological part of the book. This means that only the final portion of it takes us into the eschatological climax (just as is the case in the parallel literary structures of other series in this historical part of the book). The breaking of the first six seals thus indicates events or conditions within historical time which are preparatory to the opening of the book in judgment; these seals represent the steps or means by which God through Christ prepares the way in history for the opening and reading of the great will or book of destiny at the judgment in the eschatological consummation. The seventh seal fitly represents the silence which accompanies that opening of the will.

No part of the scroll is read in the section of Revelation from 4:1 to 8:1, a section fitly called "God Works for Man's Salvation." Events connected with the eschatological correlative must be looked for in 19:1-21:4, where God concludes His work for man's salvation, judges men from the books, and rewards men accordingly. God's downtrodden people may cry out during the historical period, "How long, O Lord, holy and true, do You not judge and avenge our blood on them that dwell on the earth?" (6:10). The response of the eschatological period is that He has judged and avenged (19:2). And as a result of judgment, those who are not found written in the "book of life" (20:15) are assigned to the lake of fire, whereas for God's children the cry issues forth, "Behold, the tabernacle of God is with men, and He will dwell with them and they shall be His people, and God Himself will be with them and be their God. And God shall wipe away all tears from their eyes; and there shall be no more death, neither sorrow, nor crying, neither shall there be any more pain: for the former things are passed away" (21:3,4).

All this is entailed in the opening of the sealed book of Revelation 5. Destiny for all men is at stake. And although the preparatory steps sometimes seem long (as evidenced by the cry already mentioned, "How long, O Lord...?"), the series of seals itself gives assurance to oppressed, discouraged Christians that God in His own good time will vindicate and reward His faithful children. The message of the seals is akin to that of II Peter 3:9-13:

> The Lord is not slack concerning his promise, as some men count slackness; but is longsuffering toward us, not willing that any should perish, but that

all should come to repentance. But the day of the Lord will come as a thief in the night; in which the heavens will pass away with great noise and the elements melt in fervent heat. The earth also and its works shall be consumed. . . . Nevertheless we, in harmony with His promise, look for new heavens and a new earth, in which dwells righteousness.

The breaking of the seals must, then, be interpreted in harmony with the facts (1) that this series is in the historical part of the book and (2) that the seven-sealed scroll depicts a will or testament. Although the events described in connection with the breaking of the first six seals occur in historical time, much more than a simple description of church history is involved. To recognize that the central focus is on the steps or means which God utilizes to work for man's salvation preparatory to the opening of the "book of destiny" gives a special urgency to the message. It also gives special assurance and comfort. There is assurance that God is indeed present and at work during this historical era as the Lamb breaks the seals. And there is comfort to know that any seeming delay in the complete fulfillment of God's ultimate purpose is attributable to His longsufferingness as He uses all means possible in working for men's salvation prior to the reading of the will which reveals men's eternal destinies.

IN CONCLUSION

In the foregoing chapters I have presented a survey of various factors which must be taken into account in developing a proper hermeneutic for understanding and interpreting the book of Revelation. The emphasis has been on literary features and concerns related to them, an aspect of the subject which has been quite generally neglected. Interpretation has not been given, but it is hoped that the guidelines I have presented will provide help toward more clear and consistent interpretation—interpretation which will bring to the fore the fact that the book of Revelation is "large with immortality" and which will give due prominence to the twofold theme of God's presence with His children even now in their trials and of His final reward for them when the prayer is answered, "Even so, come, Lord Jesus." Above all, it is hoped that as these guidelines are utilized, the resulting interpretation will be such as to provide a message which has relevance for the crying needs of our own day—a meaningful and helpful message which brings encouragement and inspiration as it furnishes vital glimpses of "the open gates of heaven."

APPENDIX

ESSAY I

COMMENTARIES BY LEON MORRIS
AND GEORGE ELDON LADD

This brief essay takes cognizance of two rather important commentaries on the book of Revelation which have appeared since the manuscript for the first edition of *The Open Gates of Heaven* was prepared: Leon Morris, *The Revelation of St. John: An Introduction and Commentary* (Tyndale Bible Commentaries, New Testament Series, Vol. 20; Grand Rapids, Mich., 1969); and George Eldon Ladd, *A Commentary on the Revelation of John* (Grand Rapids, Mich., 1972). Both are by distinguished New Testament scholars, whose competence in the field is recognized and who manifest in their commentaries a wide knowledge of the relevant literature, both ancient and modern.

I

Morris' publication has been described in a bibliographical notation in Ladd's book (page 298) as combining "the preterist and futurist views," but a careful reading of the work itself leaves the impression that it contains little, if any, characteristically futurist interpretation. The point of interest to us here, however, is not the interpretational stance of this commentary, but rather the attention it gives to literary analysis of the book of Revelation. Unfortunately, there is no discussion of this matter in Morris' Introduction (pages 15-41), which gives particularly good coverage to a number of other items. But in outline form a detailed "Analysis" of the Revelation is furnished (pages 43, 44), and this does indicate the author's care in considering literary structure. The major divisions in his outline are as follows (excluding the Prologue and Epilogue):

The Letters to the Churches	2:1-3:22
A Vision of Heaven	4:1-11
The Seven Seals	5:1-8:5
The Seven Trumpets	8:6-11:19
Seven Significant Signs	12:1-14:20
The Seven Last Plagues	15:1-16:21
The Triumph of Almighty God	17:1-20:15
A New Heaven and a New Earth	21:1-22:5

63

II

Ladd's commentary deserves a special degree of attention, not only because the author has distinguished himself by a number of competent studies in the field of eschatology and apocalyptic, but also because his book represents the first full-scale attempt to treat the Revelation from a futuristic standpoint of non-dispensationalist variety (at least on the American scene in recent years). In his Introduction Ladd states his belief that "the correct method of interpreting the Revelation is a blending of the preterist and the futurist methods" (page 14). However, in the applications or interpretations which he makes throughout this commentary, very few reveal any serious preterism except perhaps for those relating to the material in the first three chapters of Revelation. The messages to the seven churches in Revelation 2 and 3 are treated as applying to John's day. Thereafter preterist-type references are few and cursory; and especially beginning with the 7th Seal (Revelation 8:1), the basic applications are made in a futuristic sense (see pages 110, 121-123). The touches of any genuine preterism in this commentary seem to be so slight that I have chosen to classify the publication as a "futurist" work rather than as representing a "blending of the preterist and the futurist methods."

Ladd's treatment of literary structure, futhermore, is also characteristically futuristic. His outline on pages 15-17 is fortunately quite detailed, but his actual discussion of literary structure in his Introduction is limited to this brief remark on page 14:

> In terms of literary structure, the book consists of four visions, each of which is introduced by an invitation to "come and see" what God purposes to disclose (1:9; 4:1; 17:1; 21:9). The book is concluded by an epilogue.

One could well compare this fourfold division with that indicated or implied in the treatment recently given the book of Revelation by an outstanding exponent of the dispensationalist position, John F. Walvoord, *The Revelation of Jesus Christ* (Chicago, 1966). Comparison could also readily be made with the literary structure provided by Merrill C. Tenney, to which I have called attention above, on pages 33, 34. For the sake of convenience my summary of Tenney's outline as given on page 34 is repeated here alongside that of Ladd's (in each instance only the four main divisions are noted, and the Prologue and Epilogue are excluded):

TENNEY		LADD	
Christ in the Church	1:9-3:22	The First Vision	1:9-3:22
Christ in the Cosmos	4:1-16:21	The Second Vision	4:1-16:21
Christ in Conquest	17:1-21:8	The Third Vision	17:1-21:8
Christ in Consummation	21:9-22:5	The Fourth Vision: The	
		Heavenly Jerusalem	21:9-22:5

It should be noted that Ladd's stated basis for his four main sections—the repeated phrase "come and see" in the book of Revelation in conjunction with "what God purposes to disclose"—is considerably less elaborate than Tenney's reasons which I have summarized on page 34. My concern expressed there that Tenney has oversimplified the literary aspects of the book of Revelation and developed his outline on a rather artificial basis applies even more strongly to the work of Ladd.

Although Ladd utilizes a typically futurist outline for the major sections of the book of Revelation, he breaks with the common dispensationalist interpretation in several major respects, some of which he specifically notes on page 12 of his Introduction. We may list the following: (1) He rejects the concept of a "secret rapture" of the church prior to the visible second coming of Christ; (2) he "finds no reason . . . to distinguish sharply between Israel and the church," the church being the group who face "fearful persecution" (page 12); (3) he does not see in the letters to the seven churches "a forecast of seven ages of church history" (page 12); and (4) he defers his strictly futuristic application until the 7th seal of Revelation 8:1 instead of beginning it at Revelation 4:1, as dispensationalists generally do (he treats the intervening material after the letters to the seven churches as covering the Christian era in a sort of "philosophy-of-history" manner).

Concerning the third point above, it is fair to say that although dispensationalists tend to interpret the seven letters as depicting successive epochs of church history, they do not always limit their interpretation to this. One could well note, for example, Walvoord's comments on pages 50-100 of his afore-mentioned publication, where this writer gives recognition to the seven letters as applicable to John's time, plus reckoning with the possibility of periods of church history.

Ladd's commentary, in my opinion, is one of the best available as far as futurist-oriented commentaries are concerned. Nevertheless, it suffers from various weaknesses which futurist interpreters hold in common (see my main text above, page 12). Futhermore, it would appear that Ladd creates certain difficulties of his own.

It is not my intent here to present a comprehensive review of Ladd's commentary, but it is appropriate to call attention to several anomalies which seem related to his particular analysis of the literary structure of the book of Revelation:

1. His second major section, from 4:1 to 16:21, seems awkward in relationship to the application he makes of the material in the book of Revelation. The first portion of this major section, up to the 7th seal of 8:1, he applies, as already noted above, to the current Christian era, and then he suddenly breaks into his "futuristic" type of interpretation for events that he believes are to occur during a relatively short period of time prior to Christ's second advent (see pages 110, 123). However, this sort of application does not stop at 16:21 but continues on to 19:10 (see pages 245, 252). Thus one would assume that a more appropriate and logical division for Ladd to have used should have been 8:1-19:10 instead of 4:1-16:21 if his interpretation is correct. There somehow seems to be a clash between his outline and his application of the materials in the book of Revelation.

2. Ladd's division of Revelation overlooks the importance of the literary technique which structures a similarity between the trumpets and plagues and also a similarity between chapters 12-14 and 17, 18. On the basis of indications within the Biblical text itself I have suggested that these parallels signify historical and eschatological correlatives (see pages 46 and 47, above). Ladd, however, arranges one item after another from 8:1-19:10 in a generally chronological sequence which obscures the parallelisms and leaves unanswered the question of why, from a literary standpoint, John has provided them.

3. Nevertheless, Ladd does suggest some parallelisms which involve the seals, trumpets, and plagues. For one thing, there are *interludes* between the 6th and 7th seals and again between the 6th and 7th trumpets; and second, the 7th seal and 7th trumpet *lack content* (see pages 121, 122, in his commentary). In his generally chronological outline of futuristic events from Revelation 8:1 through 19:10, he finds that "neither the seventh seal nor the seventh trumpet represents a plague or a woe as do the other six seals and trumpets," the content of the 7th seal being found in the 7 trumpets and the content of the 7th trumpet being found in the 7 bowls or last plagues (see page 122). Several questions may be raised about Ladd's suggested parallelisms here: (1) The interludes he notes, and which are indeed present in the Biblical text, do not have a further counterpart between the 6th and 7th plagues. For his particular sequence this would seem to be an omission; for he includes the plagues in the same main literary section as the seals and trumpets, and he also finds that the plagues, like the seals and

trumpets, are "poured out upon mankind before they are overtaken in the final judgment and it is too late" (page 122). (2) Chapters 12-14 of Revelation become, in Ladd's outline, an interlude which is unusual indeed. It has no parallel elsewhere in the book, and both its positioning and length are most awkward in that it creates a break between the 7th trumpet and that trumpet's supposed content in the 7 bowls or last plagues. (3) Ladd's contention that the 7th seal and 7th trumpet lack content—the content of them being found in the 7 trumpets and 7 bowls, respectively—is his own assumption and cannot be deduced from the book of Revelation. The so-called "interlude" of Revelation 12-14, to which I have just called attention above, should have given warning of something wrong. However, there is more to say: The 7th seal of Revelation 8:1 does *indeed* have content when the "silence" mentioned in it is understood in the context of a courtroom scene where a will or testament is being opened (see my comments about this on page 57, above). Likewise, the 7th trumpet of Revelation 11:15-18 does indeed have content as revealed in the various declarations made in that passage, including those which relate to judgment, to reward for God's servants, and to destruction of the "destroyers of the earth." To say, as Ladd does, that there is no "woe" in the 7th trumpet contradicts the most obvious reading of the text (what worse woe could there be for the evil forces than their final judgment and destruction?). Ladd misses the content of this 7th trumpet because he interprets that content as being a proleptic announcement. One may well wonder if such use of prolepsis has not arisen here unconsciously as the child of an exegetical dilemma—a dilemma which has come about because of a preconceived pattern or outline that does not allow for "content" in the 7th trumpet.

4. The apparent historical allusions in Revelation 12 also disrupt the pattern or sequence of futuristically interpreted events which Ladd sees from Revelation 8:1 through 19:10. These allusions seem to fit past history, and for chapter 12 Ladd suddenly utilizes a "mythical language" approach in his interpretation. For example, the reference in 12:5 to the birth of the "man child" whom the dragon sought to devour and who was "caught up to God and to His throne" are statements that, according to Ladd (pages 169, 170), do "not refer to the birth of Jesus" and "can hardly be an allusion to the ascension of Christ." But what solid justification is there for use of a *different interpretational method* for chapter 12 from that which is utilized prior to and after this chapter?

Further interpretational difficulties could be cited, of course; but no attempt has been made to be exhaustive. On the other hand, I wish to state emphatically that there is no intent, either, to belittle the painstaking work of a serious scholar. And there is no doubt but that Ladd is painstaking, serious, and competent. Even though interpretationally I must differ radically with him in many places, I can recommend his book for its wealth of background information on various points of the Revelation. Nevertheless, this important publication illustrates only too well, in my opinion, the very real danger that confronts even the most competent and conscientious of scholars when literary features are given insufficient attention as to their hermeneutical import.

Indeed, Ladd's commentary suffers from a problem too common among both futurist and "straight-line" continuous-historical interpreters: failure to allow the book of Revelation itself to speak adequately from the standpoint of its literary structure. "Recapitulationist" continuous-historical interpreters and "philosophy-of-history" interpreters tend to do somewhat better in this respect.

In closing, it is worth emphasizing again that the book of Revelation must be studied in the context of its literary milieu and with due regard for its own literary features (see especially Chapters II, III, and V, above). Such study is primary to the interpretational stance to be taken, and concerns of the kind just mentioned must be allowed to lead to the mode of interpretation used, not *vice versa.*

ESSAY II

PAUL MINEAR'S CONTRIBUTIONS TO A STUDY
OF THE BOOK OF REVELATION

In the main text of the present book I have twice referred to important work done by Paul S. Minear: on page 30 and again on page 40. The latter of these references calls attention to his recent volume entitled *I Saw a New Earth.* Because of the special significance of this publication, my critical review of it which appeared in *Andrews University Seminary Studies,* Volume VIII (1970), pages 197-199, is here reproduced in full:

An understanding of the literary structure of the NT book of Revelation is essential to correct hermeneutics in dealing with this book. Unfortunately, such analysis of literary features is altogether too often neglected in studies of the Revelation. *I Saw a New Earth* is different. One of its truly strong points is that it gives extensive and careful attention to literary features as well as to historical backgrounds.

This publication contains three major parts: (1) "The Visions" (pp. 1-197); (2) "Issues in Interpretation" (pp. 199-298); and (3) "Translation with Annotations" (pp. 299-365). There is a bibliography (pp. 367-384), but no index.

Part I contains a section-by-section presentation of Minear's own translation of the Apocalypse. Following the translation, there is an analysis of the literary structure of each section, consideration of special items for discussion and reflection, and notation of points for further study. Helpful bibliographical references are given in connection with the points for further study. The sections into which Part I is divided are as follows: "The Triple Introduction," "The Promise of Victory," "The Lamb as Victor," "The Prophets as Victors," "The Faithful as Victors," "Victory over Babylon," "Victory over the Devil," and "The Triple Conclusion."

Part II, "Issues in Interpretation," includes the following nine chapters: "The Significance of Suffering," "The Prophet's Motives," "Sovereignties in Conflict," "The Kings of the Earth," "Death and Resurrection of the Sea-Beast," "The Earth," "Heaven," The Clouds of Heaven," and "Comparable Patterns of Thought in Luke's Gospel." These are all stimulating and challenging studies. Often they touch on points which are quite debatable. The final chapter is particularly interesting to the present reviewer because of its abundance of evidence marshalled against a current trend to treat the book of Revelation as unlike the rest of NT thinking. Minear has chosen Luke's Gospel for this study because it supposedly is the furthest from John's mode of thinking, and he has done well in proving a similarity.

It may seem unusual and redundant that a translation of the Revelation should be given twice in this publication—first section-by-section in Part I, and then as a whole in Part III. However, in this particular work it is a happy choice that this is so. The repetition of the translation provides a better overview of the Revelation and enables the reader to grasp more readily the totality of that book's message. At the same time, this second presentation of the text affords the author opportunity to add extensive annotations which would have been cumbersome if attached to the translation and discussion given in Part I.

Minear's literary treatment is twofold. Not only does he analyze the literary structure of the book of Revelation section by section, but he provides his translation in a typographical arrangement which makes literary features stand out. Of this typographical arrangement he himself says that it "is designed to break up long prose paragraphs and to free readers from the lock-step of verses and chapters. The arrangement of the material may also help one to visualize basic units of thought and symmetries of structure. It separates narrative from dialogue and clarifies the roles of various actors and speakers" (p. xxiv).

As for the author's translation, his choice of wording may at times seem rather novel as compared with standard translations. But his is a translation worth reading. Regarding this translation he says, "In many cases the Greek text offers a plurality of nuances which justify various renderings in English. The choosing of one of these rather than another gives a particular emphasis which may at times exclude other nuances. Yet I believe that each word of the translation chosen here is justified by the sense of the original" (*ibid.*).

The interpretational perspective from which Minear views the book of Revelation is interesting. He does not deny "the urgency with which John was addressing himself to a specific situation," but he also finds "continuing relevance" of John's message (see *e.g.*, p. 127). His approach is what I would call "philosophy-of-history," though I do not know whether this term is one which Minear himself would use to describe his perspective.

A pivotal interpretational point at which many, including this reviewer, will differ from Minear is his tendency to apply the various warnings and judgments of Revelation as being directed against Christians. As Myles M. Bourke points out in his "Foreword" to Minear's book, "If I have not misread Dr. Minear, one of his major preoccupations is to show that the tribulations sent upon men in the three visions of the seals, the trumpets, and the bowls, and also the punishments spoken of in Vision 4 . . . are not primarily, and surely not exclusively, punishments of the Church's persecutors, but of

Christians who are in one way or other faithless to their vocation"
(p. ix). To this view Bourke himself takes exception on various grounds
(see pp. ix-xiii).

On the other hand, one must admire Minear's effort to break with
the common view that the apocalyptic and prophetic literatures of the
Bible are poles apart, the former being a prime example of hate literature whereas strong ethical appeal is characteristic of the latter.
This view, which provides a deep cleavage between apocalyptic and
prophetic, has, of course, been competently attacked also by Amos
N. Wilder. However, the fact that the Apocalypse is not a "revenge
missive" does not necessarily lead to the conclusion that the judgments
described in that book must be intended for the church rather than
for the church's persecutors.

It should be added that Minear's position regarding apostate
Christians as constituting the target for judgments depicted in the
Revelation is not simply an *a priori* deduction; rather, it seems to stem
from his evaluation of internal data. In addition to what he says in *I
Saw a New Earth* itself, his brief treatment of the matter in an article
entitled "Ontology and Ecclesiology in the Apocalypse," *New Testament
Studies*, XII (1966), pages 89-105, also deserves notice. In the part of
this article which deals with the question in hand, he has taken
particular note of the hortatory thrust of the Revelation (especially in
the seven letters of chapters 2 and 3, but also in items elsewhere) and
has coupled this thrust with the catalogue of negatives in Revelation
21:8. This list of negatives, he declares, "is a summary of typical actions
against which John was exhorting the churches" (page 101). And as he
says later, "John's concern throughout is with the behaviour of persecuted insiders, not persecuting outsiders" (page 102).

In view of this, it seems logical to conclude that the judgments
reflected in the book of Revelation are indeed primarily against apostate
Christians—specifically, Christians who have fallen away from among
God's people whom John is addressing. Nevertheless, several basic
considerations must be kept in mind in evaluating Minear's conclusion:

1. The fact that the book of Revelation is epistolary (in addition
to being apocalyptic) would sufficiently account for the hortatory thrust
in it. Moreover, the fact that the negatives of 21:8 seem to be
counterparts to admonitions to the churches need not necessarily suggest
that only apostate Christians are referred to in that list. It could be
taken to mean that God's people are warned against the very things
which are characteristic of *all* those whose lot will be in the "lake of fire."

2. The epistolary nature of the book of Revelation must not be allowed to obscure its characteristics as a piece of apocalyptic literature, nor to detract from its own stated theme. Apocalyptic is designed to give hope to God's people, especially in times of distress. It does so by drawing back the curtain, as it were, to reveal God's care for His children in spite of current obstacles and hardships and to give them assurance regarding the future day when all things will be set right. This ties in beautifully with the twin theme of the book of Revelation itself as announced both in its prologue and in its epilogue (see my treatment of this twin theme on pages 43 and 44, above).

3. In speaking hope to God's people, apocalyptic makes a clear division between two opposing sides—the forces of good (God and His people) and the forces of evil (Satan and his cohorts). The fact that the book of Revelation rebukes Christians for faults, warns them against apostasy, and appeals to them to endure—whichever the case may require—does not mean that the division mentioned above is drawn between only Christians themselves according to their response to the exhortations given. Rather, it appears that the lines have *already* been drawn between the two opposing sides, and that the appeals to God's people are made in order to guide them to be on the right side.

4. In the original setting of John's time, the basic persecuting forces represented in Revelation 13 are considered to be imperial Rome and the cult of *Roma et Augustus*—forces which are certainly not addressed by John as part of the constituency of the seven churches. It does seem, of course, that "false Jews" (2:9 and 3:9) and even such apostatizing Christians as the followers of Jezebel (2:20-23) might either join or lend their support to the persecutors of God's people. I would concur with Minear's conclusion in *I Saw a New Earth* that to limit the application to the historical situation of John's day would be too restrictive; but nevertheless any further applications, it seems to me, must be true to what the original setting implies. After the "Christianizing" of western Europe, the composition of the beast powers of Revelation 13 might change; but these powers must still represent Satan's evil forces in contrast to the Christians to whom the book of Revelation is addressed.

In addition to the foregoing points, consideration should be given, of course, to the various arguments provided by Myles M. Bourke in his "Foreword" to Minear's *I Saw a New Earth*. Among such arguments are the fact that it would be difficult to equate the "kings, potentates, generals," *et cetera*, of Revelation 6:15 with faithless Christians of the first century, and the fact that the tribulations of the trumpets and bowls do not seem to be trials which have as their purpose the separating of faithful Christians from faithless ones (pp. xi, xii). Bourke points out that the intended object or target of these trumpet and bowl tribulations are the "earth-dwellers," who have been identified in Revelation 6:10 as those who have slaughtered the Christian martyrs (p. xii). He notes too that most of the bowls have as their model the plagues on the ancient Egyptians—calamities from which the Hebrews were spared—, and he queries as to whether not some conclusion can be drawn from this as to whom John meant when speaking of the victims of the plagues of the bowl vision (pp. xii, xiii). Furthermore, although calling attention to the authentic Christian tone in Minear's reluctance to allow severe judgment on "the outsiders" while permitting such for faithless Christians (on the basis that "from him to whom much has been given much will be required"), he raises question about whether John would have looked upon the pagan persecutors of the Church as acting in good faith and in ignorance of the maliciousness of their deeds (p. xiii). In introducing this last item, Bourke has drawn attention, it might be added, to the fact that the Revelation stands in the tradition of apocalyptic and that the portrayal of destruction of the enemies of God's people as given in literature of this type does not, in his opinion, come "far short of Christian standards"; in fact, he refers specifically to the New Testament's similar interpretation concerning the fall of Jerusalem (p. xiii).

In conclusion, it is worth mentioning that Minear's article on "Ontology and Ecclesiology in the Apocalypse" brings to attention some very significant material regarding hermeneutical concerns that are often overlooked by scholars. Minear immediately places himself "on the side of the philosophers who believe that as biblical historians we should do more than we have done by way of clarifying the ontological outlook of biblical authors" (page 89). His review of the data regarding what he terms five cities or places either indicated or implied in Revelation 11 as in opposition to God—Sodom, Egypt, Babylon, Jerusalem, and Rome (see pages 94, 95)—is most helpful. These places are drawn together as John saw the story of each of the five "as fully historical, and yet as fully eschatological"; for him "space functioned in such a way as to unite Sodom and Rome, not to separate them" (page 96). This is a "comprehensive rather than a disjunctive mode of seeing and thinking," apprehending events "in terms of their inner structure as responses to God's action. God's action in each epoch induced a recognizable pattern of reactions, and the prophet sought to discern that pattern for the sake of his readers" (page 96).

What Minear has called to attention in the preceding paragraph is akin to, or at least parallels, my own brief discussion of the Biblical theme of "God being ever the same" on page 21, above, and particularly what is added to that discussion in footnote 4 on pages 21 and 22. It also relates well to the concept of "fluidity of symbol" mentioned on page 28.

ESSAY III

SOME FURTHER EXAMPLES OF LITERARY ANALYSIS

Various sorts of outlines of the book of Revelation were called to attention in Chapter IV, but brief reference will be made to several other types here. Two in particular will be illustrated: (1) a kind that compares the sequence of messages in the Revelation with those in another Bible book, and (2) a kind that reveals chiastic structure. The latter has already been illustrated, of course, by my own new analysis set forth in Chapter V, but one further illustration will be furnished in the present essay.

To illustrate the first category, I present below (in parallel columns for easy reference) the outlines comparing Ezekiel and the Revelation given by T. F. Glasson, *The Revelation of John* (Cambridge, Engl., 1965), pages 12-13. Glasson's work is particularly interesting in view of the Revelation's close conceptual relationship to the book of Ezekiel.

Ezekiel	*Revelation*
(1) Ezekiel in captivity sees a vision of God (ch. 1).	(1) John in captivity sees a vision of Christ (ch. 1).
(2) Messages to the Jewish people (chs. 2-24).	(2) Messages to the seven churches (chs. 2-3).
(3) Judgements upon the nations (chs. 25-32).	(3) A series of judgements (chs. 6-19) (introduced by visions of God in chs. 4-5).
(4) The Messianic kingdom (chs. 33-37).	(4) The Messianic kingdom (20:1-6).
(5) The attack of Gog (chs. 38-39).	(5) The attack of Gog and Magog (20:7-10), followed by the Last Judgement (20:11-15).
(6) A vision of the final glory and peace of the redeemed people of the Lord, closing with the words, "The Lord is there." (chs. 40-48).	(6) A vision of the final glory and peace of the redeemed people of the Lord in the new Jerusalem. . . ."God himself shall be with them." (chs. 21-22).

Conceptually similar to Glasson's approach are analyses that parallel the sequence of messages in the Revelation with the content of the "Synoptic Apocalypse" of Matthew 24, Mark 13, Luke 21 (see, for example, Alfred Wikenhauser, *Offenbarung des Johannes* [3d verb. Aufl.; Regensburg,

1959 (c. 1958)] , and Austin Farrer, *The Revelation of St. John the Divine* [Oxford, 1964]).

The second approach to the Revelation to which I wish to call further attention here is illustrated by Nils Wilhelm Lund in his *Studies in the Book of Revelation,* a volume published posthumously in 1955 (Lund had given some attention to the structure of the Revelation in earlier works as well). As noted above, Lund's analysis, like my own, reveals the use of chiasmus. The beginning of my detailed study of the Apocalypse antedated by several years the appearance of this major publication of Lund's, and his results and mine were reached independently. When his work came to my notice, I was naturally much interested, especially in view of the fact that to my knowledge it is the only other major attempt to set forth a chiastic structure as underlying the entire Apocalypse. Lund's diagrammatic outline of the book of Revelation as given on page 27 of his *Studies in the Book of Revelation* is presented in abbreviated form below, on page 77.

Lund wisely endeavored to do his literary analysis on the basis of the content of the Apocalypse itself, rather than on the basis of some particular scheme of interpretation of that book. However, as we notice his results we can wonder whether he has been entirely successful. For example, his paralleling of "the little book" in chapter 10:1—11 with "the two beasts" in chapter 13:1—18 can hardly depend on literary parallels in the text, but seems rather to derive from Lund's concept that the first message is "testimony to the empire" and the latter is "persecution by the empire." Likewise, we may ask on what grounds "the two witnesses" of 11:1—13 and "the dragon and the woman" in 12:1—17 can be considered counterparts, except on the basis of this scholar's own deduction that the former represents "testimony to Judaism" and the latter portrays "persecution by Judaism."

Lund's great amount of careful work must not be minimized; but nonetheless, valid question can be raised as to whether the chiastic pattern he has portrayed rests always on the text itself rather than on an interpretation of the text.

Although further outlines or diagrams will not be presented here, attention should be called to the work of a few other scholars who have analyzed the structure of the book of Revelation. One special type of analysis, represented by several investigators, lays particular emphasis on the concept of *time* in the Apocalypse. In this vein, for example, Elisabeth Fiorenza in her "The Eschatology and Composition of the Apocalypse," *CBQ* 30 (1968): 537—569, has developed an outline on the basis of what

LUND'S ANALYSIS OF CHIASTIC STRUCTURE IN THE BOOK OF REVELATION

(Adapted from: Nils Wilhelm Lund, *Studies in the Book of Revelation* [Chicago, 1955], page 27)

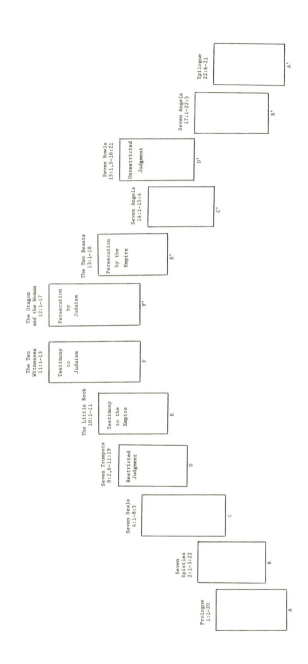

she conceives as three main themes in the book of Revelation: (1) "the establishment of the Kingdom of God and Christ in judgment of the world"; (2) "the imminent expectation, which knows only a short duration of time until the end"; and (3) "the prophetic interpretation of the present situation of the Christian community" (page 560; for the actual outline, see page 561). What may perhaps be called the beginnings of a chiastic structure may be seen in her arrangement, for she refers to both 1:1–8 and 22:6–21 as the "Epistolary Frame" (roughly comparable to what I have designated as "Prologue" and "Epilogue"), and she parallels 1:9–3:22 with 21:1–22:5 as the "Community under Judgment" and the "Eschatological Salvation of the Community & the World," respectively. The lengthy middle section of her outline, from 4:1 through 20:15, is concerned with the "little while" until the end. It contains three main subsections: "Judgment of the Cosmos" (basically seals, trumpets, and bowls), "The Community and its Oppressors (a time & times & half a time)," and "Judgment of the Powers hostile to God" (page 561).

Several years before Fiorenza's publication, Mathias Rissi had indicated a somewhat similar division of the contents of the Apocalypse (see pages 14–16 in his *Time and History* [Richmond, Virginia, 1966], a translation of his *Was ist und was geschehen soll danach* [Zurich, 1965]). First he indicates, on pages 14–15, that the "text of the Revelation divides itself into three major groups": (1) the "message to the seven churches" (chapters 1–3), (2) the "vision groups" all terminating with a "portrayal of the End of this aeon" (4:1–19:10); and (3) the "visions and sayings, which embrace the development of the coming of the kingdom of God after the great Parousia scene of 19:11ff." (19:11–22:21). Then in outline form, on pages 15–16, he proceeds to sketch the "overall plan" of the Revelation under the following four major headings: "Message to the seven churches" (chapters 1–3), (2) "Visions of the End time" (4:1–19:10), (3) "The return of Christ" (19:11–20:15), and (4) "The new creation" (21:1–22:21).

Both of the two foregoing analyses of Rissi and Fiorenza envisage that a lengthy major section of the Revelation begins at 4:1 (4:1–19:10 for Rissi and 4:1–20:15 for Fiorenza). More recently, however, Fiorenza has provided a somewhat different scheme in her "Composition and Structure in the Book of Revelation," *CBQ* 39 (1977): 344-366. After alluding to several types of structural elements which she feels are pertinent (including a reference to the actantial model), she portrays on page 364 a concentric-symmetry pattern that has as its centerpiece 10:1–15:4 (but excluding

11:15−19 and 15:1). Three sections precede this centerpiece: (A) 1:1−8; (B) 1:9−3:22; (C) 4:1−9:21, 11:15−19. And correspondingly, three sections follow it: (C′) 15:1, 5−19:10; (B′) 19:11−22:9; (A′) 22:10−21.

Vernard Eller, in his *The Most Revealing Book of the Bible: Making Sense out of Revelation* (Grand Rapids, Michigan, 1974), has approached the Apocalypse in a way which bears acknowledged dependence on Rissi; but in contrast to Rissi, he has found ten main divisions in the book instead of only three or four. Indeed, the ground covered in Rissi's long central section is divided by Eller into his sections 3 through 7 and into part of section 8−all having to do with the "End-Time" or "Events of the End" (see the last page and the inside of the back cover of his publication).

In closing, passing mention must be made of one further careful effort at literary analysis, that of J. de Vuyst, *De structuur van de apocalyps* (Kampen, 1968). In addition to the Revelation's preliminary and concluding materials (1:1−8 and 22:12−21), the book is conceived to have two main divisions (1:9−3:22 and 4:1−22:11), the latter of which has two parts (4:1−19:10 and 19:11−22:11). The "eerste deel" of the "tweede hoofdstuk," from 4:1−19:10, obviously parallels Rissi's section entitled "Visions of the End Time," albeit from somewhat different perspective.

Note: It bears mention that a number of scholars have tended to see a major division of the book of Revelation at the turn between chapters 11 and 12, one of the most recent exponents of such a position being J. Massyngberde Ford, *Revelation*, Anchor Bible 38 (1975). From the standpoint of literary structure, however, positioning such a division here, rather than between chapters 14 and 15, creates serious difficulty. For instance, the chiasm involving the double presentation of the "Exodus from Egypt"/"Fall of Babylon" motif (see pages 46, 52, above) is ignored, and a major "break" is injected directly into the course of the first portrayal of this motif. For further description of the position and a more complete analysis of it in relationship to the thematic organization of the book of Revelation, see my "Chiastic Structure and Some Motifs in the Book of Revelation," *Andrews University Seminary Studies* 16 (1978): 401-408, especially pages 402-404. (For reference to several adherents of this position besides Ford, see the afore-mentioned article, page 402, note 6. Also compare the outlines for Hendriksen, Harrington, and Niles given on pages 35, 38-39 in the present publication.)

ESSAY IV

CHIASTIC STRUCTURE IN THE BOOK OF ZECHARIAH

By Philip Payne

Introductory Note: Chiastic structure is a feature which is familiar, of course, from the Hebrew poetry of the Old Testament, but the possibility of its occurrence in prose passages within both the Old and New Testaments has not generally received much consideration. In view of the attention given in the present volume to such a structure in the apocalyptic book of Revelation (see above, Chapter V and Essay III), it becomes a matter of interest to inquire whether chiastic structure is also discernible in other apocalyptic materials.

To be sure, recognition has occasionally been given to what appears to be a limited use of chiasmus in apocalyptic passages, such as the possible inversion of pronouns used in Daniel 11 in reference to the kings of the North and South; but relatively little attention has been given to use of chiastic structure on a broad scale in apocalyptic materials. Recently, however, the Old Testament book of Zechariah has been given this sort of attention.

In 1975 Philip Payne, building in part on Paul Lamarche's earlier work on Zechariah 9–14, prepared an outline highlighting a rather thoroughgoing chiastic structure for the entire book of Zechariah. Because of the close conceptual relationship between portions of that book and portions of the Revelation, it becomes a matter of interest to include in the present volume Payne's outline, preceded by a brief essay which Payne has especially prepared for inclusion here as an introduction to his outline. Unfortunately, space has not permitted a detailed exposition and explanation of the various individual parts of the structure (that would require a book in itself), but it is hoped that the basic guidelines given below will prove useful to the reader in his study of the intriguing (and too frequently very perplexing) book of Zechariah.

K.A.S.

The Old Testament apocalyptic book of Zechariah has long baffled interpreters by its apparently jumbled structure. However, in recent years new internal evidence has been brought to light indicating an underlying unity in design and content for the entire book. This evidence also has an important bearing on hermeneutic for accurate interpretation of the book's messages. Specifically, Paul Lamarche and Joyce Baldwin have suggested that Zechariah is an interwoven complexity of symbols and themes built on a chiastic framework.[1]

Lamarche pioneered in elucidating this chiastic structure, giving his attention to Zechariah 9-14. His analysis is, in my opinion, undeniably valid. My own study would only suggest possible shifts in textual breaks between segments in Zechariah 9-14. These differences between Lamarche's arrangement and mine are due to the difficulty of distinguishing the dividing points among many bi-element transitional texts. (My analysis, showing slight textual variation from the segments as given by Lamarche, appears in the outline at the end of this essay.)

The validity of the chiastic structure in Zechariah and evidence of use of chiasmus on three levels are aptly shown by Lamarche. Textual chiasmi can be seen in Zechariah 3:7, 7:3, and 8:2. Use of the form on the segmental or chapter level can be observed in Zechariah 14:1–15. And the sectional pattern of chiasmus is found in Zechariah 1–8 and 9–14.

To my knowledge, Joyce Baldwin has been the first to give careful attention to the chiastic structure of Zechariah 1–8. This complementing of Lamarche's study of chapters 9–14 has interesting implications for the field of Zecharian scholarship. It was only after I had laboriously developed a chiastic literary structure for Zechariah that I discovered Baldwin's contributions. My findings arose independently of hers and do not agree completely with her divisions. (For my analysis, see the outline at the end of this essay.) The difference between her analysis and mine may be due to the intricate inclusion in Zechariah 1–8 of specific names and events in history. This, to my mind, gives the first half of the book (chapters 1–8) more of an historical perspective, while its absence thereafter gives the second major section of the book (chapters 9–14) more of an eschatological thrust.

I feel that the mention of specifics in the first half indicates that that section is an apocalyptic message directed to Israelites, whereas chapters 9–14, containing more generalizations, represent the author's address to gentiles, or the nations. (There are also other evidences which support this division of one basic message delivered to two different parties.)

---

[1] Paul Lamarche, *Zechariah IX–XIV* (Paris, 1961; and Joyce Baldwin, "Haggai, Zechariah, Malachi," in *Tyndale Old Testament Commentary* (Chicago, 1972).

Both major sections of the book are composed of a double chiastic pattern, as can be seen in the chart below. It will be noted that the total chiastic structure of the book has a very symmetrical sequence.

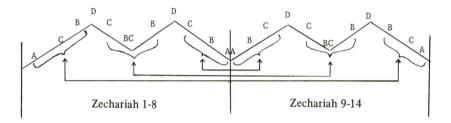

Zechariah 1-8   Zechariah 9-14

The chiastic segments of the book are based upon parallels or contrasting parallels. Clues which chiastically combine parts with their counterparts can be words, symbols, conceptual ideas, themes, or imagery. The reader who is aware of the chiastic structure can quickly see three dominant motifs, the ethical judgmental (marked by all A's and D's on the chart), the royal eschatological interventions (marked by all B's), and the martial (marked by all C's). Each segment, lettered A, B, C, D, shares certain common elements with all other segments of the same letter. Parallels and contrasts can also be found horizontally between sections, as shown on the chart by A of Zechariah 1–8 and A of Zechariah 9–14, or by A' of section 1–8 paralleled with A' of 9–14. These features are clarified on the "Tentative Outline of the Chiastic Structure of Zechariah" which appears on page 85, below.

Further study of Zechariah utilizing the chiastic structure as shown by the outline might provide hermeneutical guidelines having at least three important benefits: (1) It can serve as a check upon false interpretations and misconceptions; (2) it can act as an internal key to interpretation and Zecharian theology; and (3) it can provide a system of checks and balances by showing the internal parallels and contrasts between parts and counterparts.

The chiastic structure of Zechariah is so intricate and sublime that one can deeply appreciate it as a literary device and can recognize its contribution to apocalyptic literature. The harmonious interweaving of themes and motifs provides a vast resource for study of patterns depicting eschatology and God's intervention in human history. The only peer to Zechariah's apocalyptic style, as far as I have been able to determine, is the New Testament book of Revelation, which draws on Zechariah's terminology and perhaps on its chiastic literary structure as well.

TENTATIVE OUTLINE OF CHIASTIC STRUCTURE IN THE BOOK OF ZECHARIAH

Zechariah 1-8*

A Chastisement and Address of Salvation to Israel (1:1-6)

C Conflict and disastrous state of Israel (1:7-15)

B Return of Lord, to midst of Jerusalem and building temple (1:16-21)

D Judgement of Jerusalem, call for Israel to come out of Babylon (2:1-9)

C' Return of Lord, conflict and victorious state of Israel (2:10-13)

B' Priest Joshua, people cleansed and saved, branch (king) comes forth (3:1-8)

C'' Stone laid and victory of Israel by the Spirit (3:9-4:6)

B'' King Zerubbabel finishes the temple, stone comes forth (4:7-14)

D' Chastisement, woman captive in Babylon, judgement of wickedness (5)

C''' Conflict and victory of Israel (6:1-8)

B''' Branch crowned King, people return and cleansed (6:9-15)

A' Chastisement and Address of Salvation to Israel, Feast of Tabernacles (7,8)

Zechariah 9-14*

A Chastisement and address of Salvation to nations (8:22-9:7)

B Arrival and description of King (9:7-11)

C Conflict and victory of Israel (9:12-10:1)

D Presence of idols and false prophets, chastisement (10:2-3a)

C' Conflict and victory of Israel (10:3b-11:3)

B' Shepherd King rejected by the people, idol shepherd chosen (11:4-17)

C'' Conflict and victory of Israel (12:1-9)

B'' God's fellow King struck and pierced, mourning and purification of people (12:10-13:1)

D' Suppression of idols and false prophets (13:2-5)

B''' Shepherd, God's pierced fellow returns, testing and purification of people (13:6-9)

C''' Conflict and victory of Israel (14:1-15)

A' Chastisement and address of salvation to nations, Feast of Tabernacles (14:16-21)

*Literary structure proposed by Philip Payne, 1975.

*Paul Lamarche, *Zechariah IX-XIV* (Paris: J. Gabalda, 1961), pp. 112, 113. Translated and revised by Philip Payne, 1975.

INDEXES

The following indexes cover material in both the main text and the Appendix, *excluding* outlines and diagrams throughout the volume and also the various lists of references to the Revelation in Chapter V.

INDEX OF REFERENCES TO ANCIENT SOURCE MATERIALS
(Other Than the Book of Revelation)

Biblical Materials

Acts, 20
Chronicles, 20
Daniel, 9, 17, 19, 21, 26
Deuteronomy, 20
Ezekiel, 26, 28, 55, 75
Genesis, 28
Isaiah, 21
Jeremiah, 26, 28
Joshua, 20

Judges, 20
Kings, 20
Pentateuchal Literature, 26
I Peter, 28
II Peter, 57-58
Proverbs, 21
Psalms, 21
Zechariah, 17, 26, 55, 57, 81-84

Non-Canonical Materials

Baruch Apocalypse, 17, 20
Dead Sea Scrolls, 17
Enoch, Ethiopic, 17, 20
Enoch Literature, 17
Enoch, Slavonic, 17

Fourth Ezra, 17, 20
Jubilees, Book of, 17
Second Esdras (see Fourth Ezra)
Sibylline Oracles, 17
Testaments of the Twelve Patriarchs, 17

INDEX OF PERSONAL NAMES

Alcazar, Luis de, 11
Baldwin, Joyce, 82
Barnes, Albert, 12, 13
Beckwith, I. T., 11
Benson, E. W., 14
Bourke, Myles M., 40, 70, 72
Bowman, John Wick, 37
Bultmann, Rudolf, 30n
Calkins, Raymond, 14
Carroll, B. H., 13
Charles, R. H., 17
Clarke, Adam, 12, 13
Constantine the Great, 11, 12
Cullmann, Oscar, 10n
De Vuyst, J., 79
Eller, Vernard, 79
Elliott, E. B., 12, 13
Farrer, Austin, 76
Fiorenza, Elisabeth, 76, 78
Ford, J. Massyngberde, 79
Glasson, T. F., 75
Hanson, Paul D., 17
Harrington, Wilfrid J., 38, 79
Hendriksen, William, 13, 35-36, 79
Kepler, Thomas S., 36-37
Ladd, George E., 17, 63-68
Lamarche, Paul, 81, 82

Lohmeyer, Ernst, 37
Lund, Nils Wilhelm, 76
Milligan, William, 14
Minear, Paul S., 9, 14, 30, 38, 40, 69-74
Morris, Leon, 17, 63
Morris, S. L., 13, 14
Niles, D. T., 9, 14, 38-40, 79
Paul, Apostle, 10n, 20
Payne, Philip, 81-84
Peter, Apostle, 20
Rissi, Mathias, 78, 79
Rowley, H. H., 17
Russell, D. S., 17
Smart, James D., 21n-22n
Smith, Uriah, 13, 36
Stuart, Moses, 11
Swete, H. B., 11
Tenney, Merrill C., 33-34, 64-65
Thiele, Edwin R., 16
Wallace, Howard, 21n
Walvoord, John F., 64, 65
Waterman, LeRoy, 19
White, Ellen G., 9n, 14-16, 23n
Wikenhauser, Alfred, 75
Wilder, Amos, 17, 19n, 30n
Wright, G. E., 21n